KU-598-879

The Spirit of Natural Leadership

How to Inspire Trust, Respect and a Sense of Shared Purpose

Alison Winch

First published in 2005 by
Spiro Press
17–19 Rochester Row
London SW1P 1LA
Telephone +44 (0)870 400 1000

© Alison Winch 2005

© Typographical arrangement Spiro Press 2005

ISBN 1 84439 099 3

British Library Cataloguing-in-Publication Data.
A catalogue record for this book is available from the British Library.

Library of Congress Cataloging-in-Publication. Data on file.

All rights reserved. No part of this publication may be reproduced, stored in a retrieval
system or transmitted, in any form or by any means, electronic, mechanical, photocopy-
ing, recording and/or otherwise without the prior written permission of the publishers.
This book may not be lent, resold, hired out or otherwise disposed of by way of trade in
any form, binding or cover other than that in which it is published without the prior
written consent of the publishers.

Alison Winch asserts her moral right to be identified as the author of this work.

Spiro Press USA
3 Front Street, Suite 331
PO Box 338
Rollinsford NH 03869
USA

Typeset by: Arrowsmith, Bristol
Printed in Great Britain by: The Cromwell Press
Cover image by: Martha Holley
Cover design by: Sauce Creative Limited

Spiro Press is part of The Capita Group

For Steve, Holly and Alex who teach me about
life, love and leadership on
a daily basis

Acknowledgements

I would like to thank:

Sue Henshaw, Kellyn Reid, Pam Maberley, Lesley Mansbridge, John Newell, Anna Flint and Jane Blacketer for their unwavering belief and support.

Stewart Gilliland and Peter Radcliffe for their dedication to the real development of people, their capacity to risk and believe that there was another way in the corporate world.

Perry Wood, Paul Hunting and Elaine Harrison, the pioneers of equine-based coaching, for sharing in the magic.

Peter Maddison-Greenwell for his energy and inspiration as a horseman and a leader.

Caroline Miller Robinson for her patience in enabling me to experience moments of ultimate connection with my horse, a place I never knew existed.

Hadyn Ingram and Richard Teare who helped me connect and integrate my dreams into my work.

My friend and business partner, Jane Neil, for her unfathomable support and practical determination.

All the participants of the workshops who went to the edge of their constructs and jumped into the unknown, and to those who were willing to tell their stories.

My publisher, Susannah Lear, for her support and encouragement in bringing this book to life.

And finally, my thanks to those wonderful creatures, the horses, who offer us a window into our very souls, if we have the courage to look.

Contents

Preface

I began to write a book about leadership only to discover that it was a book about my own journey. And indeed, how could it ever be about anything else? No one can write a word that is not of their own experience, no one can utter a word that does not betray their world. There is no outside. Everything comes from the inside, no matter how hard we try to hide it, to cover it up, to objectify or rationalize it – it has still emerged from a human heart, a human mind, a human spirit. So it is with this story.

This book is not about quick fixes to the problems of organizational life – they do not exist. It is not the latest panacea for the world of leadership. It is the story of an ordinary woman of the 21st century, told from the inside of her experience as she takes her own leadership journey, reconciling and integrating all the parts of her life.

When people talk about leadership it all seems very positive, with lots of cheering from the side-lines – but the sense of struggle, of confusion, of doubt, of ridicule, of loneliness is never spoken of, only in some quiet hours, long after the event. As a woman, my unique approach to leadership was not to be found in any competency model. My apparent value was in shaping up to the male version of a leader – and for many years I did my best. After the birth of my first child, however, this became somewhat more difficult, after the birth of my second child it became practically impossible and no longer appealing. I could no longer separate parts of my self and my life.

I had to invent my own model of leadership in the modern organization, because there did not seem to be any existing model that I could follow. I did not fit.

This book is about the emergence of a different kind of leadership, one that is not about hierarchies, rules and job descriptions – one that taps into individual potential (both male and female). The book draws on my own journey of discovery and demonstrates the connection between the inner struggle and the outer action that enabled this approach to come to life. It is a human story.

The outer contribution could never have been made without the inner struggle. And for the most part we pretend to everyone else (and ourselves) that there is no inner struggle, that we are fine, we must just pull ourselves together and get on with whatever it is we are required to do – denying ourselves, our minds, our bodies, our emotions, our spirits, thinking that wanting something for ourselves alone must be selfish, rather than a cry for a meaningful life. This is how we die a little at a time. And there are millions of people in offices, factories and institutions dying a little faster than they need to, cut off from their own energy, their own emotions, silenced by the politics or the policies or the social contract – and still the screws are tightened in the name of profit, shareholder value or competition. Is that really why we toil and struggle together in organizations? Is that it?

I hate to disappoint, but I do not work for the inspiration of the beer bottle or packet of cereal on the table of a faceless consumer, or for the extra few pence dividend generated for an unknown shareholder. I work to discover the meaning for my life, measured in the depth of connection I might form with the fellow travellers that I meet along the way, and in so doing find myself.

I work to belong somewhere for a little while. I work to make my contribution to this world, somehow. And I know that I am not alone.

I have engaged with learning long enough to know that it is not the answers that I seek, but the question – because in the question is everything, your whole life is in the question, the unique question that you alone were born to live. This was mine.

Introduction

What is leadership?

What is it really?

Who are you leading?

What are you leading?

Where are you going?

Why are you going?

Who's following you?

Are they following *you* or something in you that reflects in them?

What is the nature of the relationship between the leader and the group and the time?

Why do some leaders serve in one moment and not in the next?

"People are our greatest asset", "Maximizing the human capital of organizations" – these are the words on every manager's lips... trouble is, these statements reduce us to looking at the human being through the lens of the balance sheet.

We are in a new century, a new millennium, and the speed of change in all aspects of business and life is making our existing models of being together and working together feel uncomfortable and unworkable – certainly unsustainable! It is interesting to observe that the values that operate at the subconscious level of our organizations today have more in common with the Industrial Revolution than with the requirements of the "knowledge age". They are more to do with power, process and control than flexibility and creativity. Structures are more to do with hierarchies than networks. It is clear that this traditional approach to leadership and its development is not delivering the results we seek – either in terms of business, work-life balance, health or sustainability – and yet we continue to do the same things in the same way.

So, what is the leadership required in the organizations of the 21st century? How do organizations truly unleash the potential of their leaders to create and innovate? What is the "potential" of a human being – is it some already predicted future based upon experience so far, or could there be another way? Could there be something else entirely?

New paradigms of leadership demand new methods of leadership development.

There is an emerging force in the field of leadership and team development. It is new yet touches on timeless human emotions and abilities. It is new and yet stretches back centuries to a time when horses were a fundamental part of life.

What was it that enabled the great knights of yore to ride into battle, a sword in one hand and a shield in another, with nothing other than their mental will, their very lives depending on the relationship that they had with the horse that fearlessly carried them? This relationship between man and horse was not based on fear or control, it was based on trust, respect and partnership. In this relationship leadership was a moment by moment-by-moment requirement, and your very life depended upon it.

This emerging force takes outdoor experiential leadership and team development to a whole new level, because the ropes, rafts and dead rabbits are replaced by living creatures with minds of their own – horses. Leading a horse is a whole new ball game and demands that we must first lead ourselves before we become worthy of following.

The horse is a sentient creature whose very life depends upon the signals that it picks up from its environment, and that includes signals from people. Horses translate human thoughts into actions before you even realize what you have been thinking. They provide a mirror into our unconscious strategies for dealing with relationships, business, problems and life in general. Leading a half ton of prancing stallion, that is asking you moment by moment "Are you the leader or am I?" is a new experience for most people, and only when we are on a real leadership edge such as this, when we are actually in it, can we find new resources and possibilities we never knew we had. Here is leadership and learning beyond any business model or competency framework.

This feedback can be used to generate profound transformational insights, providing many individuals with new ways to engage with their world.

This book explores leadership through the mirror of horsemanship. It contrasts the authentic "natural" leadership required by the horse against the often manufactured, synthetic, un-natural leadership of the modern organization. It recognizes that there is a new imperative in leadership that is not about leading some organization, group or team because that's what it says at the top of the job description. It recognizes that leadership is not about the size of the business, the number of people you employ or the scope of your alleged power. It is not about money, technology or big houses because in the end there is only one person that you can ever truly lead, only one, and that is yourself.

WHAT IS NATURAL LEADERSHIP?

Leadership today is not about position it is about *behaviour*. And it is only when you can lead yourself, only then can you ever hope to lead others. This "natural" leadership requires belief, trust and courage but offers congruence, alignment and access to unlimited energy, motivation and resources. It is not a leadership of control, it is a leadership of freedom and choice for yourself – and others. Because people do not follow you out of fear, you give them the freedom to follow themselves.

HOW CAN HORSES TEACH US ABOUT NATURAL LEADERSHIP?

Typically, when a "leader" from an organization meets a horse for the first time, is handed the lead rope of a halter and asked to lead the horse around the arena, they give the animal a perfunctory pat on the nose (their hand extended as far from their body as they can manage) and then march off in front of the horse. It is a matter of seconds before they reach the end of the lead rope and are pulled back suddenly by the weight of the stationary half-ton animal. Whilst there is a "marching off", generally it is accompanied by a number of anxious backward glances – all the while the leader's body language screams "I don't really mean this". There is considerable reliance on the "You are an animal, I am in charge and the one with the rope" strategy. This is then often backed up by a parental "telling off" of the horse, followed by pulling and tugging on the rope, to which the horse provides equal resistance. Next there is a request for a failsafe technique or a comment about the trouble with this particular horse. Frustration, anger, giving up, not knowing, a feeling of failure; the need to *do* more of what isn't working rather than stopping to consider whether this might be the moment of experiencing something entirely new. The unknown is a scary place. Everything the leader needs to learn is right there in that moment, in that gesture.

And on the edge of seeming failure, struggling to find a solution, stuff begins to happen. Experimentation. The coach will ask questions about the inner dialogue, the feelings in the leader's body, their emotions – what other strategies could they use to communicate with the horse? What's happening and where else does this happen? What kind of relationship do they have with the horse?

Eventually, over a period of up to 20 minutes, the leader reaches a place of stillness, a silencing of the "shoulds" and "oughts", the rules and roles, a place where they can stroke and connect with the animal – stroking its warm, silky neck; suddenly seeing its beauty, its power, its uniqueness; feeling the heat of its breath on their arm; communicating with their hands, body, energy, thoughts; creating a space in which they both want to be. Listening, responding. The leader takes a few deep breaths, into their whole body, slowly, rhythmically, easily – standing tall, projecting energy and thoughts, the leader moves forward confidently, energetically – the horse moves effortlessly *with* the leader, by their side, the rope hanging loosely between them.

The leader, when asked "What was the difference?" will think for a moment then quietly state "I just had to believe in myself", inside recognizing all the times that they hadn't believed in themselves and then all the possibilities that lay ahead now that they had.

The horse is not fooled by our pretences, our false pride. Leadership here – despite how it may appear – is not about who has the rope. The rope offers a false sense of power. The real power and possibility lies in recognizing this and reaching beyond it into fully embodied, aligned, connected, focused energy, and the ability to figure this out again and again against every new challenge. The horse demands a real leadership of self that is way beyond the level of leadership accessed in most organizational life today.

This connectivity is at the heart of natural leadership, producing a sense of effortlessness, it is using oneself in an entirely different way, a new paradigm to the striving and struggling that we know so well. It is about a focus on energy, a connection of self into the present moment as the source and place of energy; it is about the knowledge that we can create our own energy through our thoughts. It is about self-awareness, reflective learning and inner courage. Positive mental attitude is nothing new – being challenged to fully embody it and get an instantaneous measure from a horse is. This might be described as congruence, alignment, flow – an unconscious knowing that what you are doing feels right. In these moments no effort is required. When you lead in this way energy is *created* not expended. This state is characterized by centredness and focus, but also by openness to movement, change and possibility. It is independent of other people; their thoughts, their beliefs are exactly that – theirs! Natural leadership is the leadership of "magnetic attraction", you draw others with your congruence and alignment. This is not about force and control, pretence, social politeness or organizational politics, natural leadership is about the alignment of the conscious and the unconscious, the mind, body and spirit – its power is unstoppable and irresistible.

As I engaged with this kind of developmental work with horses I was astounded at the transformations that I experienced in myself and saw in others I worked with. I began to understand that the changes that were occurring were on a much deeper level than that of words alone. Emotion is always present in this kind of learning because this kind of learning is real – fully embodied, often beyond the reach of language. I wanted to understand what was happening in those moments of engagement with the horse; how could such a simple 20-minute exercise change someone's view of themselves? I was driven to take this learning method forward in an attempt to find some answers to these and deeper questions. As I continued on my quest I came to understand the dimensions of natural leadership and how you can access it – with or without a horse.

THE "KNOWLEDGE AGE"

Today we live and work in a "knowledge age". The emergence of this "knowledge age" has changed everything in the modern organization. But it has changed everything in such a way that no one has noticed! The rules have changed. The role, contribution and relationship of employees have fundamentally changed and yet we are still paying them by the hour or the week. In the knowledge age the next big market breaking idea can come from anywhere in the system, from any individual, of any age, colour, sex or religious conviction – it's not a matter of how long you have been in the business any more. In fact, by the time you "fall in line" with the company culture you could argue that you are immediately dispensable; because you are thinking within the same frames and constructs as everyone else! And then if you do happen to have an idea of some kind you will probably be told that it's not your role, not your department – send it to someone else, who does not love it or understand what it is you really mean, what you are really trying to do.

But let's just stop and consider for a moment; if we are in the knowledge age, what is it, this knowledge? Is it something, a thought, a process, that can be "downloaded" from a human being, "stored" in a computer to be called upon when it is needed? I know there are departments who actually do this. However, this model does not quite seem to hang together. Knowledge in this model is held as something that is of the intellect and written word alone, something that is static. Stuff to fill up the empty heads of new workers.

What if knowledge and knowing was an aspect of our relationships? What if it was a part of our emotions and our bodies? What if it was an aspect of different layers of consciousness? What if this is where the knowing lies? How do we put this into a computer?

IDEAS

Ideas are dependent upon people having thoughts about things that matter to them in relationships with people who are important to them. Ideas are not rational, logical processed thought. Ideas are emotions in action. They are energetic thoughts that emerge from the unique essence of a human being. Ideas come from body-minds. The stronger the emotion, the better chance an idea has. An idea cannot be separated from its source and sent off to someone else to decide whether it is worthy or not.

If an individual is not "in touch" with the well-being of their whole system, how will they produce new ideas? Well-being and optimum health may not just be a function of being able to come to work. Just because someone is there does not mean they are there! You can turn up for work and be somewhere else, as a knowledge worker. Equally, you can be anywhere else and still be making a contribution. In this sense the number of hours you attend the office may actually work against you – the more you sink into the treadmill, the narrower your vision, the fewer choices you believe you have, the more pressure you come under to produce more results, doing the same thing that isn't working.

Ideas do not necessarily need time, but they do need space. A space, a gap, a breath, an opportunity to emerge out of the busyness that is the legacy of modern life. Rushing, rushing, rushing... We need to stop and listen, to what might already be there.

RELATIONSHIPS

Ideas may be dependent upon a certain kind of relationship. Relationships are dependent upon people who care about each other, and who spend time with one another. Relationships do not depend upon structure charts, where we change the lines around into a "clearly more logical and cost-effective approach that fits our vision". In a strong relationship you can go to the edge of all that you know, leap into the midst of the half-formed crazy idea, and know that the person on the other side will catch you.

Relationships do not depend upon how people "perform". Relationships construct, nourish and grow identities. Policies are not relationships.

"Performance management" and "talent potential" ratings do not create unconditional relationships. How can someone else determine my talent and how much of it I have got when I haven't figured it out yet? There is enough judging going on in this world without institutionalizing it! Especially since most performance management approaches are built upon the idea of individual workers and their individual contribution. What, you mean this isn't the way things are? No – there is a complete blindness to the power and dynamics of human social systems, the stuff that goes on beneath the surface; the water in which we swim is invisible to us until the pond starts to dry up. This is where the real power and energy lies.

And let's face it, the pond has started to dry up. Home-working, hot-desking, mobile phones, email, virtual teams, e-learning, knowledge management, all these "technological solutions" to save time and money have instead brought a whole host of new "human" issues, and we are trying to solve them with more technology! Isolation cannot be cured with a computer. Hearts are not won by a PowerPoint presentation, even with moving graphics. Minds are not inspired by a spreadsheet. Loneliness is not removed by a mobile phone. So, if all this is saving money why are businesses collapsing? Why is the pressure to perform generating illegal and immoral behaviour? Is it just me or have we lost the plot in the modern organization?

Profit and shareholder value are held up as the gods of modern business, but these markers do not account for the invisible cost in human life-force. Profit may not be enough meaning for a life. It is not enough context for a relationship. It is not enough inspiration for an idea. There has to be something more.

The modern organization is the new community, for better or worse. This is a new paradigm, a new context for organizations. This new paradigm, this new context, needs to be supported by a new kind of sustainable "natural" leadership built upon something strong, built upon something real, built upon the only living force in organizations today – tangible human energy. Not the fancy quip, the meaningless slogan, the clean media sound bite – there is no answer, no struggle in that, it carries no real meaning.

Working with horses enables each individual to experience the subconscious energetic patterns through which they construct their world, the invisible chains that keep them bound to an inevitable course set many years before and sunk into the depths of their mind and body. All of a sudden their constructed world becomes visible, and in seeing themselves as its creator they are free to create a new world, if they so choose.

WHAT IS LEADERSHIP OF SELF, AND WHY IS LEARNING THE CORNERSTONE OF LEADERSHIP?

You will have gathered by now that natural leadership is the leadership of self and the leadership of life. There are no 10 steps to this or five answers to that.

The only way I can communicate an understanding of natural leadership and leadership of self is to look at my own journey, my experiences, the experience of friends and colleagues, the things I have learned along the way. There are no absolutes, and I make no claims to any – each of us must make our own sense of things, and ultimately take the lonely step – a step that has never been made before and cannot be found in any competency framework or business model. This is the real learning of leadership.

One thing I found when I began my quest to understand the moment with the horse, and what it had to say about leadership, was that I was not going to find the answers in the books already written about leadership, so I started in a completely different place. I followed my instincts that spoke to me of energy, physics, biology, cognition and all sorts of things that lie beneath the word and act of leadership. Some of the things I discovered rocked my world, and whichever angle I came at it from, whichever discipline I considered, all these thinkers, writers, world-renowned experts in their fields were all saying similar things.

There is a growing body of knowledge which suggests that we do not perceive an accurate, external reality through our senses or experience, but as the world famous biologist Maturana and neuroscientist Varela suggest, "we bring forth our own world" and the act of living is a cognizing act – human beings are cognizing all the time, on many different levels, whether they are aware of it or not. "The world everyone sees is not *the* world but *a* world that we bring forth with others. It compels us to see that the world will only be different if we live differently."

Think about the implications of this for a moment – we bring forth our own world; we make it up, the whole lot!

The leadership of self is a very real, literal process. We have to learn to come to the edge of our own "world", the one we have constructed for ourselves over the years, the one that guides our expectations and beliefs, the one that keeps us safe but also holds us back when confronted with a completely new, unknown experience. And when that experience is not just an intellectual one but an embodied, live, full-colour one in the shape of a half-ton horse, that edge is physical, mental and emotional. Learning here is not an informational exchange but a personal edge that incorporates emotion and energy – without this there would be no change.

Learning is the means by which we lead ourselves over that edge, the means by which we understand and assimilate the resources we found for ourselves, the means by which we re-arrange our beliefs about our possibilities in the world.

Learning is the cornerstone of natural leadership and the key to achieving your heart's desires.

Learning here is an inner directed process. We can never determine what anyone will learn because that is dependent upon the whole history of their life (which we can never know), which is why we must enable them to listen to their inner awareness, to trust in themselves as guide, because in reality there will never be another.

ACTIVATING LEARNING IN YOUR LIFE – THE LIFE-TIME NAVIGATOR

At first, as I began to talk to others (particularly in my organization) about my insights, my learning and many of the amazing people and ideas that I was running into everywhere in my life, I noticed some interesting responses. I would be talking about energy in the quantum field, or Candace Pert and her molecules of emotion, or the power of the Alexander Technique to re-align physical bodies, or the relationship between a rider and their horse. Now some people would take some of these ideas and consider them to be anything from inspirational to interesting, mildly amusing to irrelevant. So what?

Then I began to realize that I had made a fundamental error. I thought that as you came to realize that accessing what was really important to an individual was literally accessing their energy, which would then spontaneously self-generate, then if you could see this then the action that you would take was completely obvious – you would do whatever it takes to access the person – in the meeting, the one-to-one, the performance review, anywhere – you sought energy.

But no, this was not obvious. Neither was the importance of the learner having their own question, neither was sustaining a positive state, neither was paying attention to and recognizing the smallest step towards a goal, neither was deeply reflecting upon one's own thoughts.

So many of the ways in which I operated as a "learner" and a "leader" in the world were not obvious to others. This insight, as well as my research and life over the past five or so years, led me to develop The *Life-Time Navigator*, what I have come to describe as a second generation time management system – but a system that has *learning and energy* at its centre, not time and efficiency. It is a philosophy and approach that is based upon the laws of living beings, of nature, not of machines or technology. It is a system that is about unleashing human potential and supporting the individual in becoming everything that they want to become each and every day.

This book charts its emergence and underpinning ideology.

THE JOURNEY

There would be no story to tell without someone to tell it, and any story can only come from human experience. There is no outside to things; they all begin on the inside. This story is no different.

I have kept a journal since I was 15 years old. I never knew why really,

I just liked to write. Putting down my thoughts helped me process reality, to capture what I was really thinking, to just get it out. Not every day, just when I needed someone to talk to who would not judge me, who would not tell me their ideas and confuse me before I had time to figure things out for myself. Words would just pour out, raw emotion, human experience – as it was happening to me, from the middle of the experience not from the farther view of hindsight, where it can be sanitized and made fit for others. But within the words, my words, I find the human struggle, the real world that is denied on the clean, logical, bland world of organizational life. And as I have engaged with others in their own leadership and learning journeys I know that they too face the same struggles. This book contains a number of these diary entries, as well as insights, quotes and experiences from others whom I have encountered on my journey.

You may find some of what I have written very personal for a book on leadership. That is the point. This is where the real energy and emotion lies. This is where it is real. In organizational life we mostly gloss over the depths of our personalities, turn a blind eye, pretend this aspect doesn't exist – but this does not make it go away. Without access to, or awareness of, our own anguish, happiness, excitement or acceptance how can we know ourselves? If we do not know ourselves how can we learn, change or lead others? Whatever your response or reaction, there is something to learn.

Wednesday 14 May 2003

> Have completed my second "Accelerate the Capacity to Learn Programme", which was amazing. The way people can expand and all the things that I used to work so hard to install just turn up. It was wonderful. I started to shake, my teeth were chattering as I felt the energy in the room vibrate.
>
> I am spurred on to do this work as I peer into the depths of these human souls and see the anguish that is there, hidden beneath the public façade.

This is the story of leadership from the inside. Even as I write it I want to change it so that you the reader will like it more, so it might appeal to you more, the words might be better.

This is who I am. It cannot be polished up or made over. It just is what it is. And had it not been exactly so I could not have learned what I have learned. I am who I am just as you are who you are, perfectly made for your place in the world, wherever that might be. Our journey can only be to uncover what is already there and let it out.

THE WAY AHEAD

As well as describing the journey, I also highlight lessons learned – both for individuals and organizations – throughout the book. These lessons will help you, the reader:

- Assess your potential to lead in any given situation.
- Connect your inner life with your outer life.
- Create more energy for leadership in your life.
- Become motivated to lead yourself, your team and your organization.
- Create the future that you desire.

It will also help you:

- Unleash your creative and intuitive abilities.
- Accelerate your capacity to learn.
- Enhance your ability to create authentic relationships.
- Learn how to listen to yourself.
- Understand how to achieve more by doing less.
- Value your emotions as the gateway to unlimited energy.
- Know how to make real changes in your life.
- Own the self-awareness of what is truly important to you.

Bon voyage!

Waking in the Dark Wood, Where the Way Ahead was Truly Lost

The story is always within each of us, waiting to be lived, waiting to be told. The path is always silently beckoning, sometimes it is never seen, never heard and never taken, but it is always there, hidden from sight. In a sense I have, unknowingly, been following this path for all my life, guided by an invisible thread that has turned into a beacon so bright that it mesmerizes me as it draws me irresistibly forward. But it was not always so.

It was 1997 and, at 35 years old, I *was* Bridget Jones to the power of 10. I had climbed the greasy pole, and I had done it really well – as I had always done everything. I was working as a director for one of the major hotel companies, I had the company car, expenses, I stayed in the best hotel suites, I had people to do stuff for me. I had that precious thing in business known as "credibility" – *I* made stuff happen – *I* was someone! That was on the outside, on the inside…

Monday 17 March 1997

> I really need to face facts and the fact is I am deeply unhappy with this job and any days that I have that don't seem like a disaster I start to think that it's OK, but it isn't!
>
> I need some time to just think and reflect – some time to decide what it is I want to do – for me – to align my life's objectives, not just to slot into a career

and use the money to resource the things I want to do… I want real meaning in my work, I want to help others find their way…

I had my new three bedroom detached house, for which I had carefully chosen the tiles in the bathrooms and the kitchen, and I had my two cats, Tilly and Sebastian. I admit that the garden could have done with some work, but let's face it, I wasn't middle-aged yet and I might have had to get my hands dirty. I was working to become a senior manager in a large corporation; I was on a trajectory! Not only that, but after some fallow years on the relationship front I had met the man of my dreams, Steve, perfect husband material, and we were getting married in July – I mean things could not have been more perfect.

This should have given me a clue!

Anyway, Steve and I were off on holiday to Tenerife together. My period was late and for the first time in my life I had bought one of those dreaded kits. I mean, I couldn't possibly be pregnant but let's just check. I bought it at the airport, I left Steve in the check-in queue and went off to the newsagents and the bathroom. So, I got the paper and the can of Coke and went off to the loos. I will spare you the details, but there I was looking at the "windows" for the "lines" and there they were – two sets of lines – I read and re-read the instructions. The world had just changed and people were still just going to the toilet!

I got myself out of the bathroom and went to find Steve.

"Where have you been? What took you so long?" he said.

I looked at him, gave him the paper and his can of Coke and said, "You'll never guess what!"

"What?" he said.

I took my testing kit out of my bag and showed him the lines – he stared in disbelief.

Yes, I was pregnant. I mean after all those years of close calls, the bloody machinery actually worked – I was actually pregnant! I mean, with a baby! When people brought babies into work it was a standing joke, they took them right past my office – I didn't know what to do with them, I didn't even know how to pretend!

We went on holiday and I felt like I had been run over by a truck. I just wanted to sleep all the time. It's so ironic, it's the worst time of the pregnancy and you can't tell anybody. Anyway I got back home and things began to sink in.

I did not like babies. I had never had a maternal instinct in my life, I wasn't even married yet, I had my career to consider, everything I was working for was just about to turn up – it was not the time for a baby, not now.

Friday 18 April 1997

I have spent the last three weeks in trauma – I've felt a deep depression within me – escaping it to some degree at work – but it is there waiting for me at the end of every day – night time is an escape because I sleep solidly and dreamlessly from the moment my head touches the pillow – I am so tired. I have been battling with myself and that is why the conflict exists – I think – I haven't been able to hear myself – because of others and their clichés from the outside.

Meanwhile, in my corporate world, the development programmes I had just created were ready to be rolled out – five week long intensive programmes, just what every pregnant woman needs. And on the first one I discovered that my boss had invited an external consultant to sit in on my programme for a week and evaluate it, and consequently me, along with the 24 people we were already evaluating it with – just to be helpful, you understand. So I was getting feedback from anybody who looked remotely in my direction, who all had better ideas, obviously, than I had. But that was just the left hook, the body blow was to come. Just before I was to do two week long programmes, back to back, my boss told me that "unfortunately" (for whom I forget) I would not be made a senior manager at this time, despite having been promoted to the company's Executive Committee, despite succeeding at the executive assessment centre, despite leading one of the company's core strategies, the job role I was operating in was not judged to be a senior management position.

Here I was again, having to fight tooth and nail for equal recognition with my male counterparts – being bright and charismatic and leading and doing stuff, it was never quite enough. Bet that's never happened to anyone else! The last vestige of my world fell apart as I headed off to hold together these programmes for 35 company executives, for two weeks in a row.

Tuesday 13 May 1997

> I have to let go of these business perks. It feels strange – I've never chosen not to take the next step. Have I ever really made a decision in my life?
>
> I feel wafted by the winds of circumstance and what other people thought might be good for me.
>
> The highs I have had recently are all false in some sense or another.
>
> Most people would say that I should be thankful and just get on with it – I've been doing that for 12 years.

Steve and I got married in St Lucia and it was really a beautiful day in every way. My family were with me. My brother Victor from Ireland and his wife Sharon; my other brother John and his wife Kathy had come over from Canada with their daughters Kerry and Rachael, plus my goddaughter had turned up as a surprise. My best friend Lizzie, her pal Jane and my father were also there. All the important people in my life were there, apart from my mother, who had died from breast cancer a number of years previously. And really that was why I was there – being married in a traditional church wedding back home would have revealed a gap so big, a cavern so huge, I would have cried through the whole day.

You see, this is what my family was like, how my mother had created us. We are not all over each other, but there is a bond so deep and solid and unbreakable, and it holds us together over the miles that separate us. She had an ability to make each one of us feel like the most special person in the world. That was her legacy, and I was to find this again and again in many parts of my life.

Friday 5 September 1997

I am looking forward to the arrival of my child – a whole new life and generation – and a whole new phase for me, as a wife and mother. I have to admit to some trepidation but I will just try to go with the flow. I wonder what she will be like.

The programme at work is a huge success and I am leaving on a real high – I have proved once more to myself and others just what I am capable of – though, as usual, it cost me dear…

I went on maternity leave. We began to run out of money. We moved into our new house at the end of September. I sat in a chair beside the garage, directing the removal men. I decorated the baby's room with rocking horses and Billy Bond furniture. I cried a lot and missed my mother even more.

Holly Noelle Joan Winch was born on 7 December 1997, after 24 hours' labour and a caesarean section. They took her out of my stomach and wrapped her in a blanket and Steve held her up to my face. She looked at me with her big blue eyes, I said, "She's beautiful" and cried. I'll never forget that moment as long as I live. These are the moments of our life's dramas, where we are centre stage. And blow me, if the old maternal instincts didn't turn up right then! I was the calmest mother you ever came across, people would remark how calm Holly was and how calm I was – and nobody had taught me anything – I just knew stuff, instinctively. Ducks know how to swim, birds know how to fly and I knew how to be a mother. There were no competencies or job descriptions involved here, I just knew.

Sunday 4 January 1998

Holly is four weeks old today – I have survived four weeks of motherhood, Steve four weeks of fatherhood. No one tells you how hard it is. It is really tough to be on call all the time – and yet you do it calmly because you have no other option. The days blend into one another, you find it hard to remember things because your sleep is so erratic. Steve has been wonderful taking care of us both…

As time went on I began to think about the future and what I would do, now that I had a baby – my life as it was would just not work. If I went back to work full time I would lose my daughter, whom I missed if she slept for a long time! This was the paradox of motherhood, it could be really awful, but you couldn't stand to be away from them either. If I stayed at home, large parts of my life would be left incomplete, large parts *of me* would be left incomplete. All I could see was sacrifice and it was too great – how to reconcile it? Integrate it?

Wednesday 7 January 1998

> And for all this sacrifice of my family life I would get a bit more money per month and some vague idea of status – which I have learned to be empty. It still hasn't given me the ghost of success.

Over the coming winter weeks, cocooned in my lounge with daytime TV, baby on lap, I pondered how I would move my life forward, how I would integrate it. This suspended time and created an opportunity for new thoughts to emerge.

Tuesday 24 February 1998

> I am entering a new stage in my life – in a funny way I am returning to me – the me that's just me, not the me that lives through a job title and the cardboard version of what I am. This feels better, feels easier. This life holds so much less stress... I really need to decide on my priorities and align my life to them – and I must recognize that I have to let go of some things I imagine to be of some importance. I am not going any further up the business ladder – if anything I am getting off altogether – therefore I don't have to worry what anybody thinks anymore... it's great having nothing to really stress me – no deadlines to worry about, performances to agonize over – it makes such a difference to me and my life. But then again this is all just a state of mind – one that I must now control to a much greater degree.

Going through change of any kind is not as straightforward as the plans and processes upon which we build our lives would have us believe. There is much to-ing and fro-ing, much clarity and then confusion again.

Tuesday 7 April 1998

Oh I feel lost, I have spent the last two years of my life focusing on all these major events and now I don't know where I am – I don't know who I am. I don't know what I want. Everything was just so clear and now I just don't know, it's not how I thought it would be.

Tuesday 16 June 1998

I want Holly to have many experiences – ballet, music, singing, piano, gymnastics, tennis, horse-riding, bicycles – to have as much exposure to as many things as she can. To find her talents and the journey she must make.

I want to give her self-esteem, more than anything – confidence – deep down inside. I mustn't make her feel like she's looking for my approval for her decisions. She must find her own way and I must let her. There are many roads to happiness and I must let her find hers and be there to pick her up and dust her off whenever she needs me.

She really laughs at me juggling and dropping the balls, she thinks it's hysterical. She laughs at kissing noises, explosion noises and Donald Duck noises. She is now sitting up well on her own. She likes Tigger and her computer. She loves to be out and about meeting different people. She is 92nd percentile for height – and still gorgeous.

She has such a beautiful smile – she is the best of Steve and me and I know she will grow up to be a wonderful person, loved by all who meet her. How amazing to create another human being, to change the world – everything will be different because she is here.

The following months I struggled to integrate picking up my career and Holly going to nursery. It was horrendous. You hide it with the sharp business suits, the image – somehow that makes it all the harder. You are struck all the time by the paradox of motherhood and organizational life.

You pay someone else to look after your baby so you can earn money to sustain the life that you were brought up to believe was your right. I felt so cheated. No one had told me about how much I would be torn, my biological instincts screaming at what I thought I was. I had to go back, no I thought I had to go back full time in order to avoid them saying "No, we have nothing for you part-time" (this was pre-legislation) – because I did not know what to do next. And the organization was interested in applying my skills onwards and upwards.

Part of me kept getting sucked into it. I had decided by then that I would have another child because I did not want Holly to be alone in the world, and I wanted a family atmosphere like the one I had experienced growing up in Northern Ireland. I was off doing lots of different projects in the business. I was HR Special Projects, or something. And then the big job turned up – the one I had been pursuing my entire career – big salary, executive pension scheme, senior management, central London, great business – everything I had been working for – on a plate – and relocation, if I wanted it.

I saw the MD and signed the contract. And then I knew – I couldn't do it, didn't want to do it, wouldn't do it.

Here was the crossroads of my life – my outer values and my inner values had come to the point of crisis.

I called the HR Director and told her that I had changed my mind – she was not the sort of person that people said that to, so she wasn't very happy to say the least, but there you have it – possibly the first moment of personal leadership of my life.

LESSONS I HAVE LEARNED

During this time I learned that we have instincts and intuitions that we deny in ourselves as unimportant, in the depths of our minds and bodies. Denying them holds them firmly in place. Suppressing them pushes them into our bodies until they become physical manifestations of our beliefs and thoughts. Listening to them offers an opportunity to learn and trust that you know stuff that you don't know that you know!

These instincts and intuitions are the DNA of the life you were designed and destined to lead. Your feelings are real. They are important signals from your body and energy field.

Sometimes you need to get away from a prevailing context in order to see it and yourself more clearly. You need to create a clean place, uncontaminated by the subliminal energies, to think about what you need and what is going on.

No one else can know the depth of your struggle and experience, it is uniquely your own.

Only by engaging in the struggle can you get to the other side. It is part of a pattern, if you don't get over it now don't worry, you will get another chance, and another, and another – because it will keep turning up, just in different clothes.

If you hold back from it there is only a vague echo that there might be another way.

PRINCIPLES TO LIVE BY

Pay attention to your inner voice.
Write down what you are thinking.
Trust the pen, the words that come...
Trust that the stuff that turns up in your life has done so for a reason.

FOR LIFE IN ORGANIZATIONS

Organizations cannot deny the emotional life experiences of their staff. Just because it is not seen does not mean it is not there.
Policies do not assuage human experience.
The whole person is always in the room, not just the job description.
How you can begin...

EXPANDING YOUR CAPACITY TO LEARN...

Buy yourself a notebook, whatever you can afford. This is going to be your journal; this is going to be about you and your life.

Find a quiet moment in your day, a quiet space in your home, mine is usually before I go to sleep.

Put the date at the top of the page and just begin to write.

Write what you think, how you feel, and the inner voice – let it tumble out onto the page. And when you feel there's nothing more to say – just pause, listen, re-read what you have written. That will be the moment when you really listen and discover something new. Everything that comes will be important in some way otherwise it would not be present.

2

Meeting Elemental Nature in Myself

"I want to know if you have touched the centre of your own sorrow, if you have been opened by life's betrayals or have become shrivelled and closed from fear of further pain. I want to know if you can sit with pain, mine or your own, without moving to hide it or fade it or fix it."

From *The Invitation*, Oriah Mountain Dreamer

So that was a relief. I wasn't to do the "big" job in London after all. What job did I want? Staying where I was wasn't an option, apparently, even though the Managing Director would have liked me to stay and *I* wanted to stay – staying wasn't an option. This is often the logic of organizational life. The people actually involved, who at some level or another know what will work, are not the ones who make the decisions – oh no, they cannot see the long term (whatever that is!).

As for me, I just wanted to get out of the limelight, out of the way, where I could just re-group, somewhere quiet, where I could figure out what to do next. I knew of a sideways move into another division of the business, where a position was vacant. It was in a similar area, would involve no house move and I thought to myself – Let's just do that. So that was what happened.

In February 1999 I began my new role as Training and Development Manager for the Beer Division of the business. A month later I discovered

I was pregnant again. Get back on that roller-coaster, you've got another ride. It was only a matter of time before the hormones and tiredness kicked in.

Monday 12 April 1999

I am going to have to be much more honest with work about how I am feeling and what I can and cannot cope with. Really, last time a lot of what I ended up coping with was because I did not ask for help early enough – I went on being a martyr and for no reason and no one. I need to be honest with myself, be realistic but set myself some small goals to achieve each day.

I need to take life one day at a time and not think too far ahead. Put things in perspective in terms of my whole life – what's really important. And what is important is that I have a healthy child and sibling for Holly. That currently is the most important priority. Everything else takes second place to this goal. And in reality work must come pretty low on my list of priorities.

I guess what is worrying me is that people will doubt me, doubt my commitment, write me off, think less of me.

I worry as well about not coping, not coping with Holly, with keeping the house tidy, coping with work. The new job worries me, until I do something that feels worthwhile – but that is me doing that to me. Not being perfect – things feeling like a struggle, feeling pathetic… I must be aware of the stress I cause myself and stop it!

As I began to get into my job I started to run into what I perceived as other people's rules for what I was supposed to be doing, and it really started to get on my nerves!

Thursday 15 April 1999

This one director has been funny with me, I know he doesn't think much of me, I've not made the kind of impression he would like – tough! I am over everyone having to like me; I don't have the time.

I hate the office. I hate the coffee. I hate open plan and my area. I hate the car park.

I am fed up having to earn "respect" everywhere I go! I am not playing that game anymore.

Then they sold my part of the business to Belgium. Now there was no way back, no way out. The ship sailed over the far horizon and I looked around at the blokes on the life-raft and thought "Oh god!"

Thursday 3 June 1999

Life is certainly not easy at the moment. I struggle nearly all the time for a sense of balance, a sense of freedom – I do not feel I really contribute enough to my family life – to my marriage – don't feel "good enough" in these areas and I return back to my comfort areas of work.

These next few years I do need to sustain my income to get us through, especially with another maternity leave to cope with.

It's all like putting together pieces from a few different jigsaws and I can't find a way to figure it out.

Friday 25 June 1999

Each time I am away from work I feel the futility of it and the inconsequence – the hierarchies, the politics – but then I have a whole lifestyle built around what it pays – I feel trapped… I must not lose these thoughts – I talk about "my work" like what I am doing has any meaning – it hasn't – certainly not here! Happiness for me is closer than I think. I look for it in all the wrong places.

As I had entered motherhood I was confronted with the "time" issue. How on earth could I maintain the momentum of my career potential and be a mother to my daughter, who needed to be with me? And I needed her. I began to seek what I was describing as integration – a way to fulfil all my needs and all my potential, and not kill myself in the process. Little did I know the key was within me all along.

I had loved horses all my life. I don't know where the obsession had come from; no one in my family was remotely interested in horses. For my third birthday I got a toy horse from a family friend, kind of like a Barbie horse, called Thunderbolt. I remember sitting on the floor opening the present. It is almost the only one I remember opening in my entire childhood. And I adored him – I played with him until I was at least 15 (don't tell anybody) and he sat on my windowsill a lot longer than that. I never went to riding lessons. I was a bit afraid of the horses – they were huge. My father was an engineer and loved music, my mother was a teacher with three children and a home to run. As a child and teenager I learned the cello, which I was good at and enjoyed, but really did nothing for street credibility. I also played the piano, which I was also good at. I loved nothing more that to play in the dining room of our comfortable suburban house in Northern Ireland and imagine I was in the Albert Hall – Chopin, Mozart, Beethoven, Bach, Handel – I could play the first three bars of just about anything.

I think the first time I got on a horse was when we went on holiday to the Isle of Man. I was about seven. My mother took me pony-trekking. She had never been on a horse in her life and to my knowledge was never again but she took me and went with me because I couldn't go on my own. I remember her horse was a large bay with black mane and tail. Mine was a skewbald called Culpy. As I remember he bolted with me – that is to say he probably did a bit more trotting that I was expecting but to me it felt like bolting. Never the less, my love for horses continued to expand. And it is with much regret that I never got to tell my mother how much I loved her for this act of generosity.

If I saw a horse as we were driving along it would stand out like a beacon to me and just make my day. I loved watching westerns with my dad because of the horses. On the way to the airport there was a field with two horses in it, sometimes we would stop off and give them a sugar lump or feed them some grass. There is a photograph of me, aged eight, feeding one of these gentle giants. My father said that sometimes he came into my room to make sure I was OK and I would be making clicking noises in my sleep, like a horse trotting down a road. They were the love of my life, but were not really *in* my life, and I could not see a way for them to be in my life. Indeed I just accepted that that was just the way things were – I had not been born into a family that had anything to do with horses and that was that – we did music and engineering and teaching!

It was not until I was 29 years old that I took my first horse-riding lesson. It was February; there was snow on the ground. My horse was black and I was in a lesson with an 11-year old girl who had been riding for a few months. It was so weird, to do something completely new, on which I had nothing to build my knowledge and understanding – weird and wonderful. I was scared out of my wits for months. Riding is a whole body, physical thing – and you are not in control a lot of the time – especially when you are learning – I mean this animal has a mind of its own and knows more than I do about this situation! For anyone who has taken riding lessons the types of people that you meet are very different. They seem to be good with horses but are unable to interact very well with human beings, especially grown up ones. And as for supporting the learning process, from the learner's point of view – you must be joking. I can remember one particular lesson when my horse was not playing ball, well, I wasn't doing what I needed to do to make it play ball, because I was scared – my "sensitive" instructor came up to my horse with a whip and smacked it on the backside – it certainly moved then – and so did I. I thought to myself – Wait a minute here – I am paying this woman to do this!? I don't think so. I got off my horse and said, "I am leaving now, goodbye!"

I found a new instructor and since then I have been privileged to work and train and learn with wonderful people and horses.

I had continued to ride in between my pregnancies as much as was physically possible. Riding had become central to my life – the dream of having my own horse always top of my "if you could have anything you wanted" list.

Tuesday 31 August 1999

I remain determined to have my horse and riding as part of my life. By the time I am 40 remains my target.

Before my part of the business had been sold and I had been floated off in the life-raft, I had decided that I would begin a Masters degree. I had never had any desire to do this, but I had been using it as a strategy to set up a corporate university across the large organization that I had been a part of

– the old de-merger put paid to that plan. However, I had begun an Action Learning Masters in Learning. This meant that I could set my own curriculum, my own questions, my own agenda – that appealed to me a great deal. My only small problem was what would I do the Masters on now and how would I do it with an 18-month old toddler *and* a baby on the way *and* a full-time job that I was just six months into – out with the red pants and the rope of truth, I hear you say!

Things were not going well. They were, as far as I was concerned, getting worse.

Monday 13 September 1999

The picture in this business is becoming clearer and clearer to me, as to the barriers and reasons. It is a feudal system run by men. There is little place for women, especially women who are mothers and do not pretend to be men. Sure there are some good things about it. But I don't believe really that anyone here takes me seriously and I don't know if I can truly be bothered to fix the whole thing… If the organization will not let me be successful (on my terms) I will not blame myself for it. I will look for my small wins. I need leadership and there just feels like a complete lack of it – just egos tripping over each other.

My second maternity leave was fast approaching, the birth, about six weeks away. In the end I went to a conference at Henley and four days later I was back in labour. And off we went again. I was to learn another lesson – that what people say is going to happen usually has very little to do with reality. I had decided that I would try for a "natural" birth. I thought to myself – OK, and if the worst comes to the worst, I can cope with the pain if I have an epidural. I did last time.

So off we went, Steve and I in the dead of night.

After 15 hours of labour I ended up having another c-section.

I remember the nurse putting the mask to my face and giving me something to stop me being sick, then pressing lightly on my throat. The last thing I remember is looking up at the huge lights in the theatre, wondering when I would go to sleep and feeling like I was in my own episode of "ER". Next thing I knew I was coming round and the midwife was there. I asked her if I had had a boy or a girl, she didn't know, she had just come on duty. They wheeled me round to the ward where Steve was sitting with a baby. I asked him – was it a boy or a girl. He didn't hear me – I asked again – he said "a little girl", and I got my first sight of her. Alexandra Elizabeth Winch entered our lives.

Thursday 25 November 1999

I feel really happy and content with my life. I am becoming a little more laid back and relaxed. I am entering a new phase of my life – my life as a wife and mother – I now I have been doing this for a while, but somehow it seems for real now – the things I am working towards are for the family – not for myself any more. And it's not just about money as a measure of success any more.

I remember going to these meetings in America with a large hotel company that I worked for and looking at the hands of the glamorous women, seeing the rings that told me they had other lives away from work – reminding me that I didn't! That made me want to change – to have depth, to have other lives outside my work – and three years later here I am with everything I determined that I wanted – my husband, my daughters and a beautiful home. Thinking about all the adventures over the last three years, I wonder what lies ahead as we approach the 21st century. What will the rest of my 30s bring? What will my 40s bring? What do I want them to bring? Love, happiness, adventure, learning, horses – dressage, togetherness with Steve – trust and love with my daughters. I can still have my horse.

As my second maternity leave passed I was finally confronted with the fact that no matter how you looked at it you couldn't squeeze two children under two and a half and a marriage and a home into a weekend, and I realized that I would have to work just three days or so a week.

I remember watching an episode of *ER* (my favourite hospital drama on TV). It was the one where Mark's father tells him that he has cancer and Mark goes off on one saying, "Why didn't you tell me?" and all that and his father responds… "I didn't want cancer to become *my identifying feature…*" I could almost hear the penny drop, because that had begun to happen to me. I had worked in my company for almost 15 years, had a strong track record, loads of people knew of me and my work – and now when they met me the second thing they would say to me was… "and you're working part time now… " as if I just turned up for coffee mornings or something – it had become my identifying feature to some people – that really hacked me off! If there's something that really annoys me it's feeling like somebody's put me in a box, labelled it and put it on a shelf in their mind, in a spot I don't want to be!

Monday 3 April 2000

First day back at work – I feel just awful – and it's like a ball of string that I can't find the end of it.

Is it just too soon? Is she too young? She has a cold.

The business and the lack of success I feel there? Not doing the corporate university? All the judgements?

My feelings about my children and motherhood have shifted – I want to be a big part of their lives – I want to be the one with them every day – they will grow up so quickly – the work doesn't really matter to me. My career doesn't. What matters to me is to feel as though I am learning and innovating, That's where I get the buzz, and all this against the family value, programmed into me at such an early age I don't remember any other way, that you don't give up, no matter what the cost… All I know is I feel raw, I feel emotionally volatile a lot of the time. I feel tired, letting everyone down – I can't win. Where am I going? What do I want to do?

Those early days back at work were a living nightmare. I had little sleep on top of little sleep, struggling to figure out what I was going to do with this bloody business, and my immediate team, none of whom had children and so no inkling of how it might be for me, and who had a list of expectations the length of your arm, the only one of which I fulfilled was "turning up", and I only did that three days a week!

Sunday 23 April 2000

I am a bundle of raw emotions at the moment – I am completely exhausted – it's 9.30pm and I am in bed – I am constantly tired – I wake up tired. I am frustrated at getting through the bare minimum to live, never mind anything else. Life is so hard for us at the moment – so draining. Sometimes I feel empty – there's nothing left – and then I remember something else I haven't done, or someone else's birthday I have forgotten. Getting back to work is hard – at times almost unbearable. Contradictions and irony, that is what life is made of, tricks and surprises… I feel so much at the moment – I feel everything – I guess that's my hormones. I did not realize how much emotions play in my identity but they are a big part of what makes me, me. I still have so many dreams… so much I want from this life. Holly chirps in the room next door – she is so bright and clever – she is mesmerizing. Alex is almost sitting up and just as bright. I am rich in my daughters. They are beautiful and smart. I wonder what they will do and what they will be… as I learn to be their mother every day.

Tuesday 25 April 2000

I stumble from day to day. It's 9.50pm; Holly is still awake. Alex has gone to sleep (for how long?). I've been up since 7.00am – I am exhausted, I feel inadequate in most aspects of my life – as a mother – Holly is distant from me, and I am so worried that I will lose Alex too. When you've been away from her she doesn't see you for a while once you're back. She's going to nursery next week and it's breaking my heart. I go from moments of joy to anger to loneliness to envy to confusion, frustration and all the while exhaustion. There is no one that wants to listen because there is no way to sort it out.

I constantly feel like resigning. I cannot make this business work for me. I find it hard to accept myself sometimes.

Tuesday 2 May 2000

Another day – and I climb into bed exhausted, torn apart, frustrated, and generally feeling my life doesn't work. There is only so much of me – and I cannot keep stretching.

I cannot cope with this business any more. Maybe it's all in my imagination, I don't know, but for whatever reason I just can't stay there – I could offer something but I'd have to work so hard to do it, and I am not prepared to. I want to enjoy my children, and everything takes me away. I can't cope at home either, with no support from anywhere.

I have some stuff in my head I need to sort out. I am going through a fundamental values conflict.

Work alienates me completely – the beer, the football, the culture, the whole thing is completely male orientated and macho!

And I, with all that is happening to me and all that I am becoming, do not fit there any more – well, I never did.

I don't know how to make things better – it's all a ball of string and I can't find if it's one piece of string or lots of bits of string.

Seeing Lizzie was great – like drinking from a well.

I'm so tired all the time – always feel not good enough – like someone else would be managing things better.

Wednesday 3 May 2000

Am having a really hard time with Alex going to nursery – no, not her, me – I feel so... I don't know. I imagine her face and I have to get to her immediately. I miss her. I feel guilty about everything. I try to be logical and positive but I just keep feeling so desperate, as though I can't cope and am failing everyone. And I'm tired.

I have my girls; I want to be with them. I don't want to get home at 7.00pm in the evening.

Sometimes I can't even express myself. I need to talk to someone. I just feel like running away from work.

Monday 15 May 2000

Life goes from hard to very hard to awful. I am not getting enough sleep and the weekends seem relentless. Then I get stressed out about the house not being tidy. I lost it yesterday – a combination of my hormones and relentless days. I need to figure out what to do…

Thursday 8 June 2000

Horse-riding tomorrow, fantastic! I can't wait – Eva is such a great teacher. I am so glad to have that piece of my life back again.

Wednesday 28 June 2000

The awful thing is that as much as I rant and rave about the problems at work, they are probably of my own making based on my models, not others. I am going to have to redefine my model of success. And my model is of a busy person, on the phone, who is valued by the MD and keeps getting stars, and because I can't do that I am not doing anything.

What I have to recognize is that this model does not work for me or the business – it's old, 1980s, and does not serve. I need a new model that is more about others – helping others succeed.

I need to recognize that my life has changed beyond all recognition and I cannot be the old person any more. I am struggling to find this new one, I am struggling to find my place in this business – perhaps I need to listen more, go and see more people, ask more questions rather than being so concerned with having answers to protect myself and be fighting and railing all the time. I need to communicate more, I am facing jumps and I am going around them. Changing everything around me will not change this.

So, a plan:

Let go of things a bit more.

Focus on others and how they are feeling but don't own their problems.

Set up a plan to take learning forward in the business.

Stop negative powerless thoughts – I have as much or as little power as I take, not what is given to me (just like horse-riding).

Use Kellyn and my team more – lead and manage, focus and don't be afraid.

All this will be a start. I have got to take control – I am being a victim.

This state continued for some time. As I rewrite these pages and re-access those experiences I notice how so often we hold developmental breakthroughs as kind of "done", that's it, over. But it just does not work that way. First there is the very real struggle that is going on in your life for a long time, it feels never ending and inescapable, it's like you go to the edge of the cliff and look over and say – "Oh my god" – it's worse than that, it's an abyss.

But only by going to the edge can you get the merest glimpse of something else, a glimmer of light, a new way through. And as you focus upon it, it gets bigger and you can figure out new ways to do things. But it is still not done because this new insight has to almost re-wire your neurology – it has to re-cast everything else. And not only do you need to do that, you also have to physically embody the change you want to make. You have to take it from a thought, late at night in your bedroom, out into the cold light of day, and demonstrate it to other people, before you are even sure of it yourself.

So despite this small breakthrough in the fog of my life I continued the never-ending struggle, but it had changed in some small, but significant way, that I only see now, as I look back.

Saturday 22 July 2000

I'm not even sure who I am these days – this new identity.

I wish I didn't take life so seriously. I wish I could let go a bit more – make it more of a game – work – that is…

Horse-riding this week has been fantastic. I loved it! I want more of that in my life.

How am I ever going to get this Masters done?

I really need to figure out what I want in my everyday life and how I want it to be because this is all there is. And if being happy daily is important then I have to sort a few things out – because there is a gap!

It is only two and a bit years and I will be 40. It's hard to believe. Almost the halfway stage of my life – I really must make the most of every day.

How to enjoy all the moments, the little things, and eliminate the irritants – stop doing things that make me feel bad – do stuff that makes me feel good. Be with people that make me feel good! Not put pressure on myself – just be!

Sunday 27 August 2000

Life is full of paradox. Lots of change – deep change – children and marriage being the greatest changes but they are hidden in the hurry and burry of everyday life. But they change the fabric of your relationships and therefore you – my relationships with my father, my brothers, my friends, my work. I notice that I am always talking about getting my life "back" – but this is my life, now, this everyday "busyness" of daily living – not the escape from it. And when I am in it, I like it. I have enjoyed this week with the children. I am closer to Holly. I don't have enough time with her – you don't realize it until you do have the time...

I need to become this new version of me now – a more integrated version, taking things as they are, not thinking how they should be, measuring the gaps and focusing on that. Think about how far we've come and go from there, just like riding. Chill out more about things that don't really matter. Look farther ahead at the overall direction I want to go and make the shifts.

My children are bright, beautiful, funny, engaging, intelligent and loveable – they are truly wonderful and I know this will multiply over the years to come. They will be the punctuation of my life from now on. Riding will help me grow; it holds such parallels for my life and my possibilities...

When you sit on a horse everything that you are is present in that moment, conscious and unconscious, every belief fully embodied. Emotionally, mentally and physically leading in the relationship with the horse demands a quiet faith and confidence in self, above everything and everyone else. This is the beginning of leadership, beginning to turn to the inner struggles as the source of the outer problems.

I began to read because of my Masters degree. It had taken me some time but I had finally figured out what question I wanted to ask. And considering I had spent 16 years or so in Human Resources type jobs and I was, in fact, the Training and Development Manager, it was a funny question.

It was this – "How do people learn?"

I had been assuming that I had known the answer to this question, but I was wrong. I had been looking at the whole e-learning thing, how technology-driven knowledge and skills were going to revolutionize the world of training, how we were going to know how many hours' training people had taken, and what their test scores were and what the skill gaps were – I mean I was going to have real power!

But then as I actually sat down and did some of this e-leaning stuff. I couldn't pay attention for longer than 10 minutes and that was a stretch! I don't know whose questions they were answering because they weren't mine. And it was so slow and BORING. And these e-learning companies were trying to tell me that for a mere £200,000 I could give all the employees in my business access to this kind of learning.

Funny thing was when I asked them my question, the old "How do people learn anyway?" question, they just looked at me blankly – they could tell me how the technology worked, but somehow the argument as to how the people in my business were going to be transformed didn't quite hang together. That's when I knew I was on to something!

So I began to read everything that gave a hint of something that might help me address my question. It was so exciting – like being a detective.

I was off sick for a few days and I had obtained a book that a friend of mine had been raving about, *Seeing Systems* by Barry Oshry.

As I read this book I experienced the first of many seismic shifts that would occur in the fabric of my world as I began to engage with my quest to try and understand how people learn – because the heart of that question was not only about other people, it was also about me and how I come to terms with my life.

Wednesday 4 October 2000

How liberating to understand that many of the feelings I have had in organizational life have been about the dynamics – and not about me, good or bad – I am not a function of organizational dynamics alone, I operate within them, but they are not me, nor do they define me any more.

In essence, the Oshry book was saying that human beings tend to operate in social patterns below the level of conscious awareness and that, in any relationship, we will occupy one of three spaces – top, middle or bottom – and that each of these spaces has distinct characteristics. Over time we develop certain responses to the different "spaces" we occupy – it's like a kind of dance that develops, only we don't realize that we are dancing and that our every gesture is a response to the "space", not necessarily the person who seems to be causing our angst, which we experience as personal.

A whole different paradigm emerged in every aspect of my life. Each space has its advantages and disadvantages, but the power was in realizing that they existed at all, and understanding that there were opportunities to lead at every level. A new way of looking at people and performance and learning in organizations was presented, and it definitely had nothing to do with e-learning. The most critical aspect of this discovery, however, was the Eureka moment that exploded in my body – these spaces were exactly what I had been experiencing in the business. I was in "middle" space – with its characteristics of being torn and isolated, with no one else who shared my goals because they all their own stuff to do. The biggest thing of all was that it wasn't about me, personally, after all – it was the space and now I could do something about it!

I finished the book that day and could not stop talking about it to everyone I met.

This discovery was not enough to save me from a presentation that I had to give to the board on "The People and Organization Review" – an overview of the people and succession plans in the business. I had spent months preparing this report and presentation and had ignored the fact that I did not feel comfortable about its purpose, its process, why we did it at all! However, I did what you often do in these situations – I did it anyway to the best of my ability. This was in the middle of a great deal of business uncertainty and the board were waiting to hear if the company was to be, well, dissolved – so it wasn't a great day to be doing a presentation! On top of that, I was late – the motorway I took to work was gridlocked as usual. I rang ahead to say that I would be late – and I was first on the agenda. I rang the MD's secretary, but of course, she wasn't there and the MD picked up the phone. He was a reasonable guy and I explained that I would be late in the way that you do when you are trying really hard to pretend that you are totally cool about the whole thing but inside your breakfast is doing somersaults. And he sounds like this is about as important to him as who wrote the 1812 overture.

Finally I got there, totally flustered, with no time to take a breath, and had to go straight into the presentation. From the first slide things began to fall apart – they didn't like the words I used... what I had put in my presentation was not, despite the fact it had come from them, accurate... it was a disaster. I had never felt so humiliated in my life. There I stood before this huge round table, in this darkened room with all these deep, critical voices destroying every slide I presented, as I tried to act as though I did not want the floor to open up and swallow me.

Wednesday 8 November 2000

I am angry – angry about work – anger from failing... angry at myself and angry at everyone around me.

I hate these "leaders" – I don't want to build relationships with them – I don't want to pander to their egos any more – if they want something they should come and find me!

I have so much to add and they cannot see beyond their own paradigms. I feel like I have hit a downer. I heard Tan, a colleague, talking to her mum on the phone – you can talk to your mum in the way you can talk to no one else.

How can it be that 10 years after her death I miss her as much as if she had just died? Maybe I have a form of depression – I had a week feeling up and now I'm down again.

I want to cry and scream and howl but nothing will come – I want Steve to hold me and tell me it will all be OK – I want my mother.

I don't want to pretend any more, I don't want to be afraid any more, I don't want to be excluded any more.

Sunday 3 December 2000

Friday would have been mum's 65th birthday.

I am finding life really tough at the moment – overwhelmingly tough – and I keep trying to find some answer, some solution – but nothing seems to work. I feel so inadequate as a mother – I feel all sorts of things I am not supposed to feel. I feel so trapped all the time. I just run around all day after the children – I hate it – and I'm "supposed" to love it, and I don't. I get depressed, I can't cope, I get angry – at my lot, and the lot of thousands of women like me, I guess. I am jealous of people who don't have children – their freedom, their indulgence. I resent the fact I have no relationship to speak of with my husband because we have no time together.

And all the while this daily, hourly struggle I know as life is unspoken, is plastered over with smiles and acting as though it's nothing, and it's my job to handle it anyway.

I am angry at my sex. We are cheated in so many ways. I rage at the world, at my society. Oh I know there are women worse off than me, but that does not help me.

Horse-riding is my salvation – the time when I feel I am actually achieving something.

I am changing. I have never felt such consternation, confusion, contradiction and paradox. All of this and I love my daughters fiercely.

So how do you make it work?

Whoever said life was fair?

I have to keep fighting for my dreams – I have to keep trying to figure it out. I feel like there is an answer, I just haven't found it yet.

I obviously didn't know it then, but an answer was very shortly to present itself.

LESSONS I HAVE LEARNED

When you think things can't get any worse, they invariably do.

It would seem that we are only driven to discover a new answer when we are really, really lost. And I mean it really hurts and it really matters. Otherwise where is the energy for change?

Understanding a new paradigm intellectually and translating it into our everyday life are two totally different things. Deep change can take a long time to integrate; it's not a one-time deal, it's one small step after another, wondering all the time if it's making any difference. It takes faith and commitment.

Even though we deny our emotions and instincts and intuitions, these are the elements that guide our lives.

When we are struggling with something the universe will usually provide some kind of guidance, you just have to keep an eye out for it.

Your talent in life will be so natural to you that usually you can't even see it, because to you it's so effortless it's not even worth mentioning

Human beings are social creatures, relating all the time, dancing all the time.

Doing something we love, just for the love of it, sustains us.

PRINCIPLES TO LIVE BY

You are never lost, you are always somewhere. You are somewhere and it's called "here", very close to "now".

You are "here" for a reason, to learn something you need to learn.

Pay attention to what you love to do – it's critical for your life on every level.

FOR LIFE IN ORGANIZATIONS

Special edition for board members:

When you are stand-offish, hierarchical, unwelcoming or critical of people it hurts them and they can usually do a pretty good job on this without your help.

Hurting people does not motivate them.

Is your boardroom a friendly place? (I don't mean from your point of view.) When someone uses language that you are not familiar with, perhaps they are trying to tell you something that you don't already know. This is what you are paying them for.

Just because you tell someone something and they appear to be doing it does not mean you have won or you are right. You may just be kicking the discretionary effort out of someone. This is wasting time, energy and money. The people in your company own it just as much as you do – sometimes they even care more.

EXPANDING YOUR CAPACITY TO LEARN...

Now that you are getting into writing and listening to yourself, think back over your life, as far as you can go, right back to childhood, and write a potted version of your life story, thinking about the things that shaped you, the adventures, the aspects that made you who you are today. Write it in the third person, by that I mean, I would write – Alison was born etc – as though you are talking about someone else. And again, just write what comes, without judgement – just allow it to flow.

After you have finished, take a moment to re-read what you have written and look for any patterns that you can see, consider any emotion that is created; what can you learn from your life's journey up to this moment? Write about that.

3

The Child is the Mother of the Woman

"Whatever particular horizons drew us as a child are the original patterns and templates of our adult belonging. They are clues as to how we find our measure of happiness and satisfaction in the world."

From *Crossing the Unknown Sea*, David Whyte

How many businesses do you know that "need to change their culture" and is more "change" going on than you could shake a stick at – and is anything really changing? Perhaps your company or business is going through something like this now. Do you see evidence of the change – and I don't mean a new computer system or a new business process – I mean changes in behaviours, changes in relationships, change that creates the kind of "You will never believe what so and so has just done!" effect.

Why's that then? Why is there so much talk of change and yet so little of what is predicted actually happening? Wrong level of change perhaps? And usually the "other" people have to change, those further down the hierarchy! Can you change someone else?

Our assumptions, beliefs and values have embedded themselves into our mental and physical structure. They are our roadmap for the interpretation of our world and we never really stop to question who gave us the map, whether it is the right map and whether it is getting us where we want to go. Often we are not even conscious that we are looking at a map!

We think the world in which *we* live is real, instead of constructed by us, based upon our past experience throughout our lives – it's all there. And if you think about the sheer amount of information that we have to process it's no wonder that we process much of it unconsciously, otherwise we would never get anything done. It may be that we are so efficient at learning every moment that we do not even realize that we are doing it – we are not conscious of what we are learning at all levels.

There are a number of therapies called body therapies – Rolfing and Hellerwork –where the therapist works directly on the miofacial tissues of the body – these are the fluids and tissues that run through our muscles. As they work through the tensions in the body an emotional trauma that was the original source of the tension returns to the patient's mind, to be examined and processed. When you look at a father and son, and notice that their posture is very similar, their movement is almost identical, even when the son is only five years old, it is evident that he has "learned" in his body to move the same way as his parent. We are literally learning all the time, whether we know it or not. And the unconscious mind learns with a great deal more efficiency and effectiveness than the conscious mind. This is how we acquire our beliefs and values. Not through what we are told, but through what we feel and absorb on a subconscious level. If this is how human beings learn and change, then it can be no different in organizational cultures. It's what you do that is pivotal, not what you say!

Many of our beliefs are deeply hidden – I mean in the box, locked, in a secret room at the top of the attic because they contain fears that we could not dare contemplate in the light of day – such horrors as "I am not worthy... I am not valuable... I am not lovable... I am not enough". But we cannot hide them from the horse. If we believe this of ourselves, and the horse knows this, then what is there to follow and connect with? The horse demands that we confront these demons in order to lead – and indeed people do. The point of change is a lot deeper than you think, and it's usually personal.

I can remember the moment when it struck me that riding was the key to understanding more about myself. I was sitting on top of Sydney, not the harbour but a 16 hand, chestnut gelding, and was half way around a small cross-country course during my weekly lesson. I was stuck. I was terrified. I was frozen. My voice betrayed the tears that were on the way. Here I was confronting something I didn't think I could do, right on the edge, and the feeling was just the same, except here it was physical fear. And I remember thinking in that moment that this was just a mirror for how I am in work, in life, anywhere, where I don't believe I can go any further. I went on to do a bit more cross-country jumping but it always terrified me, and what a way to learn about beliefs – if I rode towards a fence with the doubt in my mind that I would ever get over it, sure enough we stopped, or went round it, or worst of all, I would go over it by myself. It's not as if these were big fences, the horses could step over them, I could step over them – Steve just laughed when he saw the size of them – but it's different when you are careering around on half a ton of lively horseflesh.

Anyway, one day I was reading my copy of *Your Horse* magazine and there was an article about this guy who was helping people overcome their fears in riding as well as applying these breakthroughs to the rest of their life – I was so excited, someone out there thought the same as I did!

I was on maternity leave at the time, but I stored the article away for future reference.

Once back at work, and when life was just about hanging together again, I retrieved the article, called Mark (as we shall call him), and arranged to go and spend some time with him, finding out about his approach.

I trundled down to somewhere in deepest Sussex and found my way to this little cottage, thinking that perhaps this was not such a good idea after all.

I knocked on the door of this little terraced house and I met Mark, who was to play a pivotal role in my life over the next few years. I don't know what I was expecting, but as is often the case Mark looked nothing like I had imagined him. He looked like he had just escaped from Glastonbury.

He invited me in and I took a seat on the sofa. It had seen better days and the stuffing was long gone.

I was not feeling at ease. Some people would have got up and left then and there – I was used to plush hotels, with loads of people around, and here I was in this weird guy's dusty living room, telling him where I was stuck in my life!

But then again I have always been drawn to people who are a bit different and I always give them the benefit of the doubt. This had got me into trouble from time to time, but there you are… that's another story.

We spent some time at his house and then went off to a local riding school, where they let us borrow one of their horses. I got on and did some work on my canter and jumping. It was interesting and I thought that there was something in it. At that time I had two ridden sessions with Mark, which helped me with my riding and began to let me see just how the way in which I worked with the horse was a manifestation of my unconscious leadership thought patterns.

For example, on the second occasion, I was riding a horse I was not familiar with. I had a whip in each hand as this horse was not particularly inclined to going forward. I was going nowhere and I was completely reluctant to use the whips as I was afraid of the reaction I might get. So I wasn't using them and we were going nowhere – vicious circle! And hey presto, there it was – a strategy I use in relationships – if I "like them to death" they will eventually do what I want them to – not! Of course, if I give this horse one sharp smack with both whips he's going to move, and know I mean business, but then we can get on without me hassling him all the time and getting completely exhausted in the process. And there I had it, a new leadership strategy right there! Sometimes I had to exercise my energetic authority with people in order to establish the boundaries and expectations. It's not my usual approach, but it is still available to me when required.

So here I was at this stage in my life, attempting to integrate it. I had been to a couple of horse demonstrations where I had seen these guys doing the horse whispering thing – Pat Parelli and Richard Maxwell – it did indeed seem amazing. Pat Parelli would ride a horse he had only just met, bareback with no tack; and when he got on the ground it just followed him around the arena. I had never seen anything like it in my life!

After a bit of a break Mark and I started talking on the phone again. He had started to do some "natural horsemanship" and was using this in his coaching work. Natural horsemanship is based upon develop-ing a relationship with the horse in their terms, in the language of the herd – often working at liberty, with no ropes or ties of any kind on the horse. The horse's commitment to the person is based upon a relationship of trust and confidence in which the horse seems to adopt the person as their "leader". As we talked I realized that this would really open things up, as we would not have to deal with people actually having to get on a horse and ride. About this time I was trying to develop a new leadership programme in the beer business so I reckoned time for another trip to Mark. So in January 2001, I paid him a visit.

Tuesday 30 January 2001

Went to see Mark and found more than I expected. The moment when the horse, Maddie, came to me and I stroked her and talked to her was indescribable – a moment of connection – the ultimate thing for me. Mark had set me a task – to lead the horse around the arena...

I just wanted to be there with her, touching her; I wasn't fussed about anything else. Mark said; "You just wanted to be there in a nurturing relationship – it was me pushing..."

I felt in that moment a sense of peace and oneness with myself and everything else. This is crazy, but what if I did have a talent for horses? What if actually letting myself be with them, in the way I want to, allowed me to build a connection to a horse?

I have wanted this all my life. Riding was somehow secondary; it was a way to be with them. I do just like to "be" with people. That is when I am at my best in all areas of my life; connection, nurturing, discovery. Yes, I have other sides, but in the main that's what I am – also the emotion and deep thinking – I suppose I speak of connection more than communication because what I mean is beyond words, it's about a meeting of minds.

As a little girl riding terrified me; I just wanted to lead the horse around.

The relationship – that's all there is – it shapes us, defines us, sustains us; the web of relationships in which we live.

From that day I went forward and arranged a number of one-to-one meetings with the board members and senior leaders to discuss our business challenges and what they thought the leadership requirements would be going forward. I realized that I was enough for the challenges I needed to face; I had to be enough. No model, no right way to do it was going to turn up. I just had to get in there and be me to the best of my ability and shut off all my doubts about myself.

The meeting went really well – as far as I was concerned anyway – and I built a model of organizational and leadership development as I saw it – describing what the business needed to do next. The analysis of these interviews revealed a number of key pointers for the business culture, including – moving from a functionally driven business to a total business planning approach, working more in highly focused project teams fully empowered to act, gaining a better understanding of the business context and becoming part of a global marketplace.

These pointers in turn had implications for learning – "dreaming – we must get behind our real ambition, stepping outside the box. A dream is not a target. It's looking to the future and the art of the possible..." one board member said. "We must learn from failure, learn from the team and how it operated, learn across the organization..." said another.

Leadership – "We want people who excite others – they get up in the morning and think – I'll make today exciting, interesting, for my people..."

Leadership – "When is it your turn to lead? We have moved the concept of leadership from that of seniority to 'Who has the most knowledge?'"

Leadership, learning and energy were at the heart of taking the business forward, but we needed a fresh approach – a new way.

Monday 19 February 2001

Several people have told me that I have been inspirational for them in the last few weeks.

I am beginning to see what I bring to people and it is the real "me", the essence of me – an energy, a curiosity about people – and when I get the chance to just "be" that is when I am in flow.

There seem to be so many more possibilities. Because it is in the context and the connection that things happen.

I'm thinking… if there was a market… of course there's a market! You make one up! You make it happen. If I believe in it and I believe in me, then what's to stop me?

And so my dreams began to coalesce, to synthesize. Somehow this work with horses was going to be significant in my life; it was going to be the key. I just had to figure out how to access the lock and open the door.

Sunday 25 February 2001

Work is coming together nicely – if it continues in the same vein – I must communicate to increase the likelihood – get in there, plant ideas and concepts, create momentum. Trust myself.

I want to look at the Alexander Technique over the next few months and explore that a little.

As far as my career is concerned, my goal is a holistic approach to my life. I cannot compartmentalize otherwise myself and my family lose out. I want a four bedroom home, countryside, stabling for six horses and 20 acres or so… and a ménage. I want to work with NLP, learning design, transformational stuff, Parelli. Transformational – for people and consequently for organizations… and dressage. I need the resources to support this lifestyle and they cannot come from the "big job" because I would be away from my family, with no time.

I must focus on my Masters over the next few months and get it sorted. No one must distract me from this.

Maybe it's about setting up a coaching company that draws on NLP and Parelli, on Alexander and yoga and lots of other stuff. It all comes from me trying to understand my struggle and then a desire to help others in theirs.

In the business I could set up an external company to deliver this programme, others would be interested. People like to work with me. I can make things happen. Being is the key – everything comes together.

I was starting to enjoy some success at work. We had launched an Action Learning business programme with Ashridge business school, very new, on the edge. And it was receiving strong support from the board and a number of people on the programme itself. People were beginning to listen to me now, well just a few. I was convinced that the horse work was what was needed in the business, but quite how I was going to link it in and convince anybody, your guess was as good as mine! It was a bit like finding the courage to stand up, in your navy business suit, on a tube train full of people and start singing.

The universe intervened again.

One of the general managers of the breweries came to talk to me at a meeting we were both attending. He told me that he wanted to do some work on leadership for himself and did I have any ideas? He had looked around at various courses, but could find nothing that really covered what he wanted – he wanted something on inspiration. As he was speaking to me, the hairs on the back of my neck began to quiver. Brian was a respected member of the business, but also a wonderful open guy, who was already an accomplished coach. So I told him of the experiences I had had with horses and that it might be worth a go. I was being really casual, whilst inside every molecule in my body was vibrating. He said it sounded really interesting.

So it was agreed, I would set up for Brian to go and see Mark and the horses. This was to take place a couple of weeks later. After the day, I called Mark who said it had all gone very well. I phoned Brian and asked him how he had got on. He said that it was very interesting but that he needed to do some thinking; Mark had suggested that he reflect and write about what he had experienced. So he was going to do so and would send me a copy when he had finished. It was like waiting for the results of an exam. I waited and waited. Eventually, a few days later, Brian sent me an email. I had been speaking to him on the phone. I got home late that night, but at 9.30pm I hooked up my laptop and downloaded my emails. And there was the attachment from Brian. This is what it said:

> *It has taken me some time to try to fully rationalize the experience I had with the horses. I am not fully there yet, but feel able to take some key learning from the day and lay a personal plan of action for the short and medium term. I was lucky*

enough to spend the day one-to-one and this allowed me the luxury of being selfish with the experience and learning for "me", for once. Similarly, it has been important to keep "me" as the focus of my thoughts before I decide to move on to others.

So what have I learned?

I am still astonished by the results I achieved with the horses, moving from bemusement and fear to comfort and confidence in a very short time. I am still wrestling with how I achieved the success but now I accept that I don't need to know more to move forward.

Whilst the sessions in contact with the horses retain the feeling of something like a dream, the coaching sessions are very real and are where most of my revelation took place. Here I found my natural self. The person who myself, and others, are most comfortable with. The person who was always given authority and responsibility, despite his best efforts to keep his head down and avoid it in the early days. The person who was listened to and allowed to lead, despite his apparent verbal inadequacies. The person who achieved success whilst being embarrassed to be the focus of attention when recognition and rewards were handed out.

The person who became expert at learning behaviours that fit the environment before that "learned" behaviour eventually swamped "me".

I realize now that I have achieved a great deal in my role. But what we have now is a platform.

What is needed now is leadership. We are good at control but we must now focus this control on the process not the people. The people need to be shown leadership and empowered to lead others.

I have realized that my "agenda" needs to be of equal importance to that of the business and of others. I can take comfort that I will never knowingly let the business down, but in contrast understand that I have often let myself and others close to me down in the priority of needs.

What I have done and what I will do

Decide what I want to do in the next three to five years and make this at least as important as my corporate objectives. This is likely to stay personal, for now.

I have substantially increased my time out on the plant with the people.

I have organized open agenda lunches to improve my interface with shift managers and team leaders. I intend to make my beliefs and values known and begin to understand theirs.

I intend to differentiate the role of leader versus manager; each has a role and purpose but behaviour is very different.

I will personally accept and celebrate my successes and promote and encourage others to do the same with theirs.

I have started to seek out natural leaders with whom to begin to form bonds of allegiance and support. My informal discussions to date have revealed an open door and latent potential. I have had direct feedback of surprise at my openness (general managers don't normally behave like this!).

I have arranged an "away day" with my direct report executive team, a substantial part of which will be aimed at testing our leadership in its true form.

I have a clear vision that I can make a real difference, and at the same time add value for "me". I recognize that I will encounter enthusiasts, neutrals and some "terrorists", but I know I can use the enthusiasts, win over the neutrals and manage the terrorists.

I started out to stretch my thinking on leadership, only to realize that the answer was already there within me. Watch this space.

I just began to cry.

I was so overwhelmed by his words and his experience and what he had found for himself. This wonderful man, who was loved by everyone, had looked into the mirror and seen himself! But it was more than that. I was so overwhelmed because I was no longer alone, I was right; there was something here for everyone. This thing worked in a way that nothing else I had ever experienced worked. And I knew that I would find a way to take it forward.

As all this was going on I was still following the trail of my Masters. I had hooked up with a group of consultants who worked with Barry Oshry, author of *Seeing Systems – Unlocking the Mysteries of Organizational Life*. I thought – Yes, that sounds like a book for me, I've got a couple of those mysteries – and these ideas led me to another significant piece of the jigsaw that was becoming my life.

I met leadership development consultant David Rooke, who had written a book with Fisher and Torbert called *Personal and Organizational Transformations Through Action Inquiry,* and in this book he was talking about a completely different model of human development to anything I had ever heard of – but every word he spoke resonated. This book suggested that adult development went through a number of stages, just like Piaget had suggested was the case for child development. And these stages were fundamental to the way that adults made sense of their world. Like a pair of red-tinted glasses – they made everything look a bit red, but after a while you didn't notice the red anymore, until you got a pair of blue glasses and started to look through them, then everything started to look decidedly odd! I thought this was fascinating, because I definitely felt that I had different colour glasses from most of the people around me, I just had never thought of it that way. It made absolute sense. The other thing I found interesting was that if this model was in any way helpful in interpreting adult development, then competencies were definitely out the window, the whole model of human resource development that most companies on the planet were signed up to was fundamentally flawed!

Competencies are usually developed using repertory grid technique, which was originally development by George Kelly to illicit an individual's "construct model of *their* world" – it was never meant to construct an imaginary version of "the" world that everyone in an organization would then be required to live into as though it were real. But this was how it was to be used by occupational psychologists in years to come, and how it had been used by me in a previous business! A feature of this model of adult development was that the earlier stages of development could not comprehend the later stages of development. So if competencies were developed for an organization based upon individuals at a certain stage of development, then the organization was effectively halting itself at that stage. Ironically, what large organizations need is to harness the creativity and ideas of those individuals who begin to move into the post-conventional stages of development – that is to say, they begin the inner journey, where their own values and experience become more of a guiding principle than that of the collective consciousness of the group as described by Carl Jung. But at this point many of these individuals are ejected or eject themselves because they are so different from the group – an uncomfortable place to be.

David Rooke gave me a copy of his book and I devoured it. I completed the questionnaire on the model to find out which stage I might be experiencing and sent it off to him for analysis. I waited.

He called me with the results – my profile.

I was at the first stage of post-conventional leaders, a stage called the individualist.

He sent me the information and a description of the profile and, once again, I felt the isolation slip away.

	% of managers at this stage N=233 UK 1994–2000	Name	Main Focus of Awareness	Managerial Style with this Stage
Conventional	<1%	Opportunist	Focus on own immediate needs opportunities.	Short-term horizon, focus on concrete things; manipulative; deceptive; rejects feedback; externalizes blame; distrustful; fragile self-control; hostile humour; views luck as central; stereotypes; views rules as loss of freedom; punishes according to "an eye for an eye" ethic; treats what they can get away with as legitimate. Seeks personal advantage: takes an opportunity when it arises.
Conventional	2%	Diplomat	Socially expected behaviour.	Observes protocol; avoids inner and outer conflict; works to group standard; speaks in clichés and platitudes; conforms; feels shame if they violate norm; hurting others to be avoided; seeks membership, status; face-saving essential; loyalty to immediate group, not distant organization or principles. Seeks conformity and belonging. Attends to social affairs of group and individuals.

Conventional	20%	Expert	Search for expertise, improvement and efficiency.	Is completely immersed in self-referential logic of their own belief system, regarding it as the only valid way of thinking. Interested in problem solving; critical of self and others based on their belief systems; chooses efficiency over effectiveness; perfectionist; accepts feedback only from "objective" experts in their own field; dogmatic; values decisions based on incontrovertible facts; wants to stand and be unique as an expert; sense of obligation to wider, internally consistent morale order. Consistent in pursuit of improvement.
Conventional	33%	Achiever	Delivery of results by most effective means. Success.	Effectiveness and results orientated; long-term goals; future is vivid, inspiring; welcomes behavioural feedback; feels like initiator not pawn; begins to appreciate complexity of systems; seeks mutuality not hierarchy in relationships; feels guilty if does not meet own standards; blind to own shadow, to the subjectivity behind objectivity; seeks to find ways around problems in order to deliver, may be unorthodox. Takes rather than creates goals.
Post-conventional	23%	Individualist	Self, relationships and interaction with the system.	Focus on self and not goals; increased understanding of complexity systems operating and working through relationships; deepening personal relationships; takes on different role in different situations; increasingly questions own assumptions (part of rise in self-absorption) and assumptions of others; may seek changes in many life and work situations; moving to post-conventional ways of working.
Post-conventional	16%	Strategist		Recognizes importance of principle, contract, theory and judgement – not

				just rules and customs; creative at conflict resolution; process orientated as well as goal orientated; aware of paradox and contradiction; aware of links between principles, contracts, theories and judgement; aware that what one sees depends on one's world-view; high value on individuality, unique market niches, particularly historical movements; enjoys playing a variety of roles; witty, existential humour (as contrasted with prefabricated jokes); aware of dark side of power and may be tempted by it – may misuse their own abilities and manipulate others.
Post-conventional	5%	Magician	Interplay of awareness, thought, action and effect. Transforming self and others.	Seeks participation in historical/ spiritual transformations; creator of events which become mythical and reframe situations; anchoring in inclusive present, seeing the light and dark in situations; works with order and chaos; blends opposites creating "positive-sum" games; exercises own attention continually; researches interplay of institution, thought, action and effects on outside world; treats time and events as symbolic, analogical, metaphorical (not merely linear, digital, literal); involved in spiritual quest, often helps others in their life quests.

Source: The Harthill Group, 2001

Here was a lifeline for me – a way to put some sense of structure and meaning over the experiences of my world, explaining its contradictions.

Sunday 25 March 2001

In answer to one of the questions on the form – "For a woman a career is..?" I wrote "Betrayed by her biology". That is what I felt, not seeing the possibilities or what it is about being a woman that enables me to be who I am…

Myself as a woman must almost come before all others – it is fundamental to my identity – myself as feminine – my face, my body, my way of being as a woman. I need to find that again – business can feel very male – it is easy to feel that, as a woman, you don't really belong; that's why I have felt it so keenly, because I have been doing it all my life, and here it was larger than life. It was on my radar screen and so it registered really strongly.

Re-discover myself as a woman

– physically

– mentally

– emotionally

– spiritually.

Celebrate this aspect of me, the beauty of it, and the essence of it. It is the core of what enables me to be me – my emotion, my spirit…

Being a mother – caring, nurturing, building, listening, staring fascinated into the beauty of my daughters' faces – watching, holding, filling my arms, hugging me back. This is life. This is humanity, this is connection, and this is what matters.

Here was another explanation for my feelings and my life – acceptance, in a way. The discovery of this work was to become not only significant for me but also for my business. I was to use this framework in my research for my Masters degree and many others were to be offered this opportunity for acceptance, just like me.

LESSONS I HAVE LEARNED

Pay attention to the things that attract and mesmerize you, they do that for a reason, that you may not yet understand.

Pay attention to the things you struggle with, they usually contain an important answer to a deeply buried question.

The struggle, despite how it may appear, is always within you, on the inside, not on the outside – the unconscious and the conscious. It's never really about anybody else.

PRINCIPLES TO LIVE BY

You always have your own answers – inside, not outside.

Ask the questions you really want to ask.

Do new stuff.

Only by going to the edge of our constructs do we have a chance of knowing them, challenging them and changing them.

FOR LIFE IN ORGANIZATIONS

You have two choices in organizational life. You can do what everyone else thinks you should be doing and die a day at a time, or you can stop and figure out what the real job is and do that.

While you are doing this you can be sure that no one will understand you. How could they? If you are discovering something totally new to you, they are not going to know about it ("they" being other leaders and managers around you).

EXPANDING YOUR CAPACITY TO LEARN...

In your journal, go back to your childhood dreams.

What were the things that you loved as a child? That you lost yourself within? What about through your adolescence – the things that did not fit your life perhaps, or had to be a hobby because you couldn't possibly make a living out of them?

Again, just write, don't judge, just listen and remember the child that you once were – the child who just followed their own interest before society intervened and told you what your choices were.

Waiting

"Were it possible for us to see further than our knowledge reaches, and yet a little way beyond the outworks of our divining, perhaps we could endure our sadnesses with greater confidence than our joys. For they are the moment when something new has entered into us, something unknown; our feelings grow mute in shy perplexity, everything in us withdraws, a stillness comes, and the new, which no one knows, stands in the midst of it and is silent."

From *Letters to a Young Poet,* Rainer Maria Rilke

Life continued on apace. It was now June and the deadline for the completion of my Masters degree was fast approaching – like the end of August. At this point I had been doing a lot of wrestling but had written only one of six papers. Hadyn my supervisor definitely had doubts that I was going to complete it – and he wasn't the only one! However, after a moment's hesitation, I thought – I've come this far, I'm going to give it everything I've got. And off I went.

I cleared my diary from the end of July right the way through August. I really focused my energy, my attention, everything on what I was doing, what I was learning in exploring the question – "How do people really learn?" And through my reading and research I began to discover some remarkable stuff. Not only that but I was taking what these leading experts were saying and building it into my own model! I was not regurgitating other people's models of the world – I was creating my own.

I began to submit my papers – for the first one I had got a B grade, there was more structure needed. Then I submitted the next one for marking. And stone me, if it didn't come back with an A! And the following three papers all came back with A's.

I was spurred on again and again. My brain began to function in a wholly new way – everything just flowed – the way I thought, the way I wrote, the way I constructed new models of what the mysterious human process of learning was all about. The other monumental thing that emerged was that in creating a new model of learning in organizations I found for myself a completely new way to operate in the world.

As I look back at those months I notice how little time we take in the business world to really steep ourselves in the issue that we are facing – three days would be a stretch – three weeks? No, they'd lock you up and say you were wasting money – just provide them with the one page summary. But the paradox is that unless you take the time to go as deep as you need to go, to find something entirely new, then you never will – because the one page summary, written in language that is already familiar, just doesn't do it.

I began work on my final assignment. This assignment was all about looking back at the journey of the Masters degree and understanding what you had learned, where you were now, and what was going to be next.

Wednesday 25 July 2001

So for my assignment I have to consider what is next for me – I am seeking inside myself for the spark and I find the same image – kitchen table, with my girls coming home from school, chatting about the day, looking out the window to see horses grazing in the paddock, a sense of balance and completeness, warmth and connection. This does not fit anyone else's model for me – but these are the images.

I completed my assignment and yes, another A came winging back through the virtual world. As I completed that last assignment, my future life began to take shape. It came sharply into focus. I could see it, I could taste it and I knew, beyond a shadow of a doubt, that it would be so. I was left in no doubt as to my future possibilities.

During this time I was having some coaching in support of my development. At one particular coaching session I stumbled across a significant pattern in my life. I was talking with Ann, my coach, expressing my frustration with the hierarchical, unwelcoming world of my business. She asked me for an example. So I vehemently gave her an example of the hostility that I experienced through a small incident that had happened to me.

Well, I explained to her, I was walking along a corridor one day and this guy, Tim, was walking towards me. Now I didn't know him very well, but we had spent a whole day together in a group meeting so I figured that that counted as knowing someone, at least putting them in the "person you say hello to bracket" of social relationships. And he just walked past me, didn't acknowledge me, didn't speak, didn't flinch – not even an eyebrow! I couldn't believe it – what were these people like – this was the kind of thing I had to deal with! I presented this to Ann triumphantly – what do you say to that?

She said; "Did you acknowledge him?"

Ouch! She had a knack of that, Ann did, asking those awkward questions. What did she mean – did *I* acknowledge him?

There was a moment of silence.

Then she came in with the killer. "It sounds like you were waiting for him to acknowledge you."

Somebody just changed the points in my head! Waiting! Yes! *I was waiting for him to acknowledge me.*

Because the thing is "he" wasn't the only place I was waiting in my life – I was waiting everywhere, for other people to acknowledge me, to have faith in me, to believe in me, to approve of me, to understand me. You name it, I was waiting for it. Waiting for the other... Here it was in microcosm – a macro-subconscious programme that had been running my life, keeping me stuck.

Friday 27 July 2001

> I wait for everything and then I don't have to take responsibility – but give away my choice and I give away my power.
>
> I am going to stop waiting.

As it turned out, one of the ways in which I was going to stop waiting was through a focus on my Masters degree. The trail was hotting up and I was truly discovering new ideas, new ways to think, new possibilities for real learning, and consequently real change for individuals and therefore organizations.

Some of the things I came to understand were really challenging the prevailing models of management, leadership, learning and change that were everywhere I looked. Models that suggested that aspects of human behaviour could be identified and split out from one person's personality and followed like a recipe by another, to replicate the impact that that individual achieved.

The first thing that is so obvious but somehow completely forgotten is that every individual is completely unique. I mean, this is so obvious we miss it all the time. If human beings look this different on the outside, just how much more difference must there be on the inside, given their individual experiences and histories, motivations and desires? And yet most training or learning treats "delegates" like they are a homogenous group of managers or team leaders – whatever category we have put them in for our convenience – because if we had to consider the differences between them, well the whole thing would just be too complicated for words!

One of the other things I discovered was that learning was a chaotic, non-linear process – it does not conform to an input/output model – just because you tell someone something does not mean that they have learned anything. Most training and education is based on giving people answers to questions that they never asked. And the other thing is, people do not know what it is that they need to learn – if they knew that, well, they'd just go and learn it – wouldn't they? Learning is something that you recognize in hindsight – after the event – you say something like "Well that was really painful at the time, but I learned so much from it!"

What are people doing in this chaotic and non-linear process? Well they are making sense of their experience – they are fitting new information into the frameworks, information and experience that they have already had – but where does it fit? Where doesn't it fit? What do I do with the bit that is left over? Figuring this out, helping the individual make sense of it, involves helping them understand their own models of the world, most of which they are not even aware of because they are below their level of conscious awareness. So how people make meaning is fundamental to the learning process – working to some kind of a model based on a vague idea of an inert competency model was not going to generate any learning.

The main tool that we use to make meaning in our world is language. And, in a sense, through our language and speech we construct our world. Our beliefs, our values, our paradigms come tumbling out of our own mouths. And in language we use metaphor to express those things we cannot fully articulate – when we express a problem feeling like "an endless mountain that has to climbed" then we create it as a mountain whereas if we create it as "a wave that is asking to be surfed" the words and the meaning create a vast world of difference as to the energy and possibility. And we hardly ever stop to pay attention to the very words and consequently energies that are coming out of our mouths and creating our experience. What we speak, we become.

Another funny thing about real change and deep learning is that it is not usually fun, it is not entertaining, and you would much rather be anywhere else, doing anything else with anybody else! Trainers who tell you jokes and who you could "listen to all day" are entertaining you – do not confuse this with learning. They are not challenging you, taking you to the edge of your world. Learning involves confusion; it involves being lost and is a lonely place to go. It involves letting go of some things that have got you this far but now have to be jettisoned, unlearned. This is painful before it is rewarding.

If you are creating this inside organizations people get very uncomfortable because, as someone in charge of training or learning, you are supposed to make everything clear to them so there is no pain, no confusion and they are entertained at the same time – that is you take out any possibility of learning – that is not learning, that is information. And if you are not doing this – well what kind of learning professional are you?

Here's a new paradigm for you.

In my degree and my work I was trying to connect, to integrate individual and organizational learning so that the time and money that were spent on learning and development would have an impact upon business results. My problem lay with my separation of "individual and organizational" – and because I had separated them I had to find how they fitted together. But if I change the lens, the paradigm through which I look, the problem changes completely – it evaporates. If there is only the here and now, only this moment that I am experiencing, then I am the organization – the individual and the organization are one and the same.

There is only now – think about it – only this moment and then the next and the next, moment by moment – there is not some grand plan already laid out for us, there is no past, only what we make up in our heads. And yet we hardly spend any time here, in the present moment – we are off thinking about the future or ruminating over the past instead of being in the now. WOW – now there's a thought! Because if there is only now, well, that creates all sorts of opportunities! It means that you can make the future up any way you like. You can construct the past anyway you like – you get to be actor, producer, director of your own script – how much power is that?!

If you develop, the organization develops; it's as simple as that. Well, almost. The organization develops if you bring your new-found insights into the relationships you have with the people around you. If they are not spoken into a conversation then their energy remains within you, and does not have a chance to breathe new life into your work.

I developed a set of principles from my insights that were to act as a guide in my life as well as the learning and development strategy that I was developing:

- Every learner is unique.
- The individual and the organization are one and the same.

- Meaning making is fundamental and is constantly negotiated.
- "Knowledge" is dynamic and perpetually under construction.
- Learning is non-linear and chaotic.
- Learning is fundamentally linked to our identity and how we participate in the world.

I built these principles into a new approach to learning within my business.

1ST PRINCIPLE

Any training or learning offered within my business must be built upon a foundation of how human beings actually learn – not what content somebody wanted to download. It must be built on realities not paradigms.

2ND PRINCIPLE

We would work with the business and organization as a living being, a living organism, rather than through the usual metaphor of a machine or computer.

3RD PRINCIPLE

We would support leadership that was based on an approach that said, "Who are you and why should I follow you anyway?" A natural, congruent, aligned leadership. Not the leadership of positional power.

4TH PRINCIPLE

Our learning, leadership and development approach would seek to support the individual to uncover their unique contribution and discover how they could apply it within their organization or team.

5TH PRINCIPLE

You cannot make anyone learn, you cannot make anyone transform, the best you can do is create an environment in which the possibility of personal transformation might occur.

The final piece of the jigsaw was to realize that if a business was going to create a step change in its performance, then it was not going to achieve this by "pedalling the bike faster", as the saying goes. It had to be able to change gears. This meant transformation not incremental learning. By transformation I mean finding a completely new way to do something, so that you can produce 100 times more with half as much energy.

If we were going to create this kind of human performance shift we would need to have people involved in human performance who knew what they were talking about. Learning and development could no longer be a stopping off place for individuals to broaden their careers on the way to somewhere else. Learning and development needed people who were passionate about learning, so passionate about it that they actually did it themselves and did not regard it as being able to design and hold a two-day entertainment programme. Learning and development needed to climb the organizational food chain.

And finally, to those who would sell me the £200,000 system that would deliver learning – I don't think so. The only thing that delivers learning of any kind is the most sophisticated piece of wireless technology on the planet, and that is the human being. Technology was about information, access and choice – not learning. We built our own learning management system and it cost about £25,000 thank you very much.

Even as I utter the words "my Masters degree" they do not feel appropriate. This learning, this inquiry was much more than a certificate or a degree or anything with which we usually define academic achievement. This had been a real journey of discovery for me, inside and outside – aligning my inner interests and motivations behind my work – the buzz was amazing. And it really changed things for me and my team and my business. We had a deep, strong, unshakable foundation from which to go forward. We had developed a set of beliefs about *how people learn* that was now the foundation of all our work – it was no longer about the content of what was delivered in a "training" context but about what was being learned by each individual learner – the content was theirs. This changed everything.

As previously mentioned, the final piece of my degree was do a paper which was a reflection of what I had learned but also where I was now and where I was going to go in the future, and how I was going to get there. Again I was offered an opportunity to create the future.

I determined that my long-term outcome within 10 years was to undertake a doctorate in executive coaching, acquire my own horse and in the future work to release the potential of people and their organizations.

The last line of my Masters reads: "These few years will always stand out in her life as a turning point and the beginning of the integration of self."

"Action Learning", developed by under-sung genius Reg Revans, had been a life-changing experience for me, as it has been for many, many people. Action Learning was developed by Reg Revans to support adult learning in the workplace context based upon the very real questions and problems that they faced in their own life. Yes, considering theories and benchmarking is encouraged, but the process is ultimately about defining your question, developing a research or action approach, doing something, and then reflecting upon what actually happened in order to understand what to do next. It is applied learning in a business context. It teaches people to think independently and grow their own foundation based upon experience. The experience of Action Learning led me to understand completely new ways of seeing my world.

If there is only an eternal now that we construct within then every moment, conversation and challenge we meet we meet anew, with only our past patterns to support us. The degree to which we can expand our awareness, to change our patterns, to embody new possibilities, to trust ourselves will be the degree to which we lead. Leadership and learning, for me, are two sides of the same coin.

As I had finished all my stuff for my Masters, I decided I needed a little reward, since I had been working so hard. Somehow or other I had convinced Steve that it would OK for me to go away for a few days and he was up for this. I had had details of a classical dressage trainer in Portugal for a number of years, burning a hole in one of my cupboards. So I dug them out and arranged to go off to Portugal to train with Jeorge Periera for four days at the end of August.

I was to ride the horses of all horses, the Lusitano stallions, schoolmasters, who would teach me what I needed to learn. These are the horses of fairy tales, of handsome princes and charging warriors – and I was going to ride one of them!

Monday 27 August 2001

Well, here I am in Portugal, sitting by a pool. It's perfectly still, about 2.00pm in the afternoon. Three horses are visible about 50 yards away over the hedge, beyond the pool.

I had my first lesson this morning and it felt wonderful. There is so much stuff running through my mind. I was nervous, feeling a fraud, like I was not good enough for Jeorge, and yet I want to learn from him so much. I have never been on such a forward going animal. In the UK you either get obedience, you have to push all the way or you are completely out of control. This was a perfect combination.

In the traverse I need to look where I am going, bend in the direction of motion, sit back behind the movement, keep seeking bend through the neck and get my outside leg pushing the quarters across – holding the shoulder with my inside rein.

In the rising trot I need to keep my feet forward and my legs and thighs parallel to the horse, more weight into my heel, letting it just fall – then with my seat in rising trot again sitting back more and kneeling more from my knees, the rocking feeling, not the up and down sensation.

In the canter I need to really lean back so I am "sitting" on top of the horse, my legs draped around its sides, sitting lightly to the rhythm of the movement, not heavily, suspended on my stirrups.

The canter felt so light, so balanced, but it was a little hurried; I needed to collect it more – block with the rein and push…

I am even more determined now that I want to ride dressage and probably classical, with a Lusitano stallion. Clearly, though, I am going to need a more intensive action plan to achieve this. I know so little about horses, riding, tack etc compared with what is required. And I am not going to achieve it by riding Gertie once a week! I would have to train almost every day with input from an expert instructor. This all costs money that I will have to finance from somewhere. The horse will be a one-off cost, but up to £10,000, and I would need someone like Jeorge to have it for six months to train it and me. SO I have to figure out how to integrate riding more into my life.

I achieved my Masters degree, with distinction, won associate of the year and the examiner said my work was of a doctorial standard – I cannot ask for more than that. I need to use this to build upon.

Tuesday 28 August 2001

Rode the same horses today. I improved in the first lesson, my sitting trot was much better and my position in both trot and canter was much better. I had better control in the canter. Second lesson on Libral was more difficult, and Jeorge was getting frustrated with me.

It's funny, I thought my greatest challenge would be the horses but it isn't, it's the thoughts in my own mind, that I am unworthy of his teaching – I feel not a real horsewoman – someone playing at it, and this guy does this for a living! He teaches high-level people and he's having to teach me to canter – I am so embarrassed on the one hand and yet I so want to learn, I never seem to get beyond this! Am I ever going to be able to do this or will I always feel like a little schoolgirl? I feel about 10 years old. I feel he is bored teaching me. He would rather be doing anything else. I am a bit player in his main feature – one in a series of things to do. I must recognize that this is about my learning, I do not need his approval, his permission or anything.

I need to stop giving people power over me. If this is what I want for my life then that is down to me. Plenty of people will say I am mad and not good enough, well that's tough – I am stronger than that – and I have the determination to move forward.

Wednesday 29 August 2001

I am completely in love – with the horses – with all of them, Jeorge, Portugal, everything. I feel alive again. I walked up to the top stable block this evening to see the horses and it was so lovely just to be with them. It almost made me cry. They are so completely wonderful. Not completely acquiescent, so you know when you connect with them. They either like you or not. And the paces I had today – shoulder in and leg yield in trot and much better canter transition. He was with me for the first time, he was with me, he now knows how much I want to learn from him and I listen and respond. I worship this man and his horses. I am like a schoolgirl with a crush on her teacher. Here I am engaged in my passion for horses – and a man who is poetry in motion itself – harmony with the horse, the leader, knowledge, strength, connection – the combination is irresistible.

Thursday 30 August 2001

I know this is hard on Steve and my daughters, but I cannot give it up. I cannot live my life and not do this. I returned from the dream to real life, but I was even more determined, even more inspired, something was drawing me forward.

Friday 31 August 2001

Steve does not understand why I want to push myself. Indeed, I do not truly understand either – but there is something deep within me, driving me, and it will not let go. It is a space where words, soul, spirit, truth, awe actually hold some meaning for me in an ultimate sense. I know I am making it up – but that's what it means to me. It brings raw emotions to the surface – inescapable and uncontrollable – they come from nowhere. There is nothing in my life that gives me what riding does. It's more than anything I can describe. I don't need to try and understand it – perhaps this will be the one thing in my life I will not try to understand so much, and I will just allow it to be.

Monday 3 September 2001

The beginning of the day was difficult, but it got better. I still have images of sunshine, white horses, grey sweeping manes and flowing tails. The feeling of the rhythm, me moving the horse, the horse moving me – together – in the rhythm of nature, the way it has been for thousands of years.

I will do this. I will be the rider I want to be, the way I want to be, integrate the concepts I believe in. Listen to myself – my voice above all others – trust the instinct that I possess. I can feel and sense beyond words. That's what my music was about – a kinaesthetic connection. I can connect with people and animals on this deeper level – beyond words. That is why I was so emotional, because riding is a right brain activity, like music. One thing people cannot say about me is that I suppress my emotions. They are an inherent expression of who I am – happiness, depression, sadness, frustration, anger – I can do the whole range.

Learning is a fundamental building block for leadership, certainly for the leadership of self. Every moment we face, we face as a completely new moment, every instance, somehow different from the past. Even when we feel we have done something before, it won't be exactly the same as before. Learning is the process by which we find the courage to lead, to face the unknown in ourselves and trust that we can find a way through. Learning brings out the dynamic nature of leadership. Indeed, given that language is a symbolic process, the actual state of leadership and learning may be the same thing.

LESSONS I HAVE LEARNED

There is only the living moment, only now, this is fundamental to my world. Everything I bring to the moment is past history – sometimes that is helpful, many times it is not.

The past, the present and the future are all contained in the living moment.

In the living moment I can create my own future; anything that I congruently desire can be mine. The only constraint is the limit of my imagination.

The future is created one conversation at a time.

Learning is a completely natural process.

I can learn from the smallest incident – it is the key to a deeper pattern. There is no such thing as a small insight.

Aligning learning and deep personal motivations creates a powerful energy for movement and real change.

PRINCIPLES TO LIVE BY

You are choosing everything that you have in your life right now.

Everything you do makes a difference in the universe somewhere.

What is the question of your life? What is the struggle that comes back again and again?

Ask it. Live it.

Speak your dreams and make them real.

Live your dreams, one moment at a time, one small step at a time, one experience at a time, because this is all.

FOR LIFE IN ORGANIZATIONS

An organization is its relationships.

There is no point in generating new ideas if people do not have a relationship in which to speak the one they have got.

The talent question is not "Have you got any?" it is "What is it?"

My colleague John Newell would always say, "Dialogue and conversation is the narration of relationship."

Create time and space for people to create real relationships out of the empty structure charts.

EXPANDING YOUR CAPACITY TO LEARN

What are your dreams for your future?

What do you want?

Just sit and write your answer to these questions. Whatever mad, unreasonable, completely impossible outcome that your heart desires and whispers to you, that a quiet voice immediately answers "Not you, don't be ridiculous, it can't work that way". If any of that is going on then you are definitely on to something. And ask for everything. Make lists.

Take these ideas and turn them into goals.

Put them in the positive, as though there were actually happening.

Take a page for each one. Don't hold back. Be specific – if it's a new house what does it look like, feel like, how many rooms? Detail, detail, detail.

You will have a picture in your mind – get it down on paper. Timeframes? Who's there? What are you doing? What is the weather like? Really go there and experience it. Do this with every goal that you have.

Then, go back, look at each of your goals and ask yourself the question, "So, what will that get me?"

Write down the answer and ask it again; "So, what will that get me?"

Again, and again, keep going through the layers until there is no more.

This will help you understand what your goal represents to you in the living moment, because happiness is not in the object itself, it lies in what it represents to you, the experience itself. A house might represent a desire for love, connection or freedom – for everyone it is different.

By understanding your goals and the experience that they represent, the value they express for you, something really great happens. You get to live the value as you are taking a daily step towards your goals and you begin to understand that it is the value and the experience that is so much greater than the goal itself.

Make a collage, a visual representation of your life and where it is going. Pictures, words, images – programme your unconscious mind, your awareness, so that it is taking you effortlessly towards your desired future.

⑤
Listening

THE INNER JOURNEY… ONE SMALL STEP… ONE GIANT LEAP

Are you listening? No, not to me, not to them, definitely not to the FEEDBACK ON THE 360! Listen to yourself. What do you say to yourself? How do you judge yourself? How do you deny yourself? What questions do you push away and never even entertain?

In order to connect with the horse you have to first connect with yourself. To listen into the echoing silence of yourself – picking up the pieces of your self that you have long denied and put away because they did not fit what you have been told is the right model of the world. Well there's a paradox – as long as you are trying to "fit in" according to someone else's rules, never being who you really are, you will never fit in, because the only way you can fit, are designed to fit, is by being who you really are.

We have to listen, to pay attention to what we pay attention to – it's all there already – we just have to pay attention. The horse knows this – he knows authenticity, he can smell it a mile off – and he can help us find it for ourselves. Authenticity and truth are key, they offer access to alignment, energy and the unlimited resources that are your right. When you know what you want, and you can offer the horse your truth, he will offer you a connection beyond words, beyond anything you have ever experienced.

If you have been writing in your journal you will by now have started to pay attention to what you pay attention to – on the inside. Perhaps some new things, opportunities, ideas have begun to turn up in your life. Could it be that easy?

Well, kind of… it's a bit like wishing to win the lottery but never buying a ticket – the universe can only do so much! Insights, learning and creating your future involves you in actually acting upon the insights that you have had, the changes that you want to make in your life. You do have to make it happen. Sounds easy, and on one level it is, on another it can be more difficult. These patterns that have been guiding you through your life can be strong. It can feel anything from weird, uncomfortable to downright scary to push up against them, but if you are doing it for something that you truly want then you will have an energy source deep within you to draw from.

I made another visit to Mark.

After some discussion we went out to the field to bring in the horses that we would be working with. It wasn't a particularly warm day, one of those blustery, grey days. Off we went walking up the field. I always enjoy feeling the weather. I spend so much time in my car, in offices, indoors at home, that I forget the rawness of the elements, the depth of the wet grass, the unevenness of the ground, the dampness of the air as the wind whips it onto my face.

Maddie and Seren(dipity) were grazing on a knoll, in the middle of this huge field. As we walked up to them, I guess they noticed us, but did not raise their heads from the task in hand.

We then moved on from chatting generally into the work we had gone there to do. Mark asked me who or what the horses were going to represent for me. I saw them as the organization that I was trying to engage with. Mark then set me the task – he said; "You have three minutes to lead these horses through that gate", pointing to a gate which was about 35 metres away at the bottom of the field.

The horses continued to graze. My mind went off in all sorts of directions.

I began to stroke Seren. Building my relationship with her. She ate the grass.

I switched to Maddie. She ate the grass.

I was giving everything I could to build some kind of relationship with them, the task building pressure in my mind as the seconds ticked by.

It was emerging during this time that I was waiting for a signal from them, to determine whether the relationship was in place or not – some signal of connection that they would give to me… interesting!

Anyway that strategy was having no effect, and time was passing, as Mark kept reminding me.

Then I moved on to a more "forceful", "assertive" approach, or so I thought. I began to try and nudge, well more lean into and shove, Seren so that she was heading towards the gate – even though she was *still* grazing! I don't know if you have ever tried to push a horse that weighs up to a half ton, well I can tell you, it's not very effective.

By this time my time was up, the horses were still grazing and we were still in almost the exact same place that we had started. The only difference being I was feeling a combination of a failure, useless, pathetic and very frustrated.

Mark and I began to talk. He asked me to think again about the task and whether there was any other way I could lead the horses through the gate. I thought and thought and only one idea kept floating to the top of my mind. It was the very first, instantaneous thought that I had had right at the start of the session, but I had immediately dismissed it as ridiculous, and had not even bothered to complete the thought.

I thought that I could walk down the field, by myself, and that would be leading the horses through the gate. It does sound ridiculous, doesn't it? Mark said, "Well, why don't you do that?"

I huffed and puffed, what good was that going to do? It's one thing to have a ridiculous idea it's another thing to actually do it! But he insisted, and off I went.

I began to walk down the field on my own. I felt isolated, I felt alone, I felt a bit silly to be honest. It seemed like a long way and I wanted this space to be over quickly. And all the while I felt that I was failing. How could this be success? This disconnection. But there was something else, the merest suggestion of letting go of something, the merest hint of release.

I got to the gate, opened it, went through and shut it behind me.

I stood, leaning my elbows over the gate, watching Mark as he walked down the field towards me.

I didn't know what I was supposed to feel, but it wasn't successful, happy or anything that fell into a category like that.

Mark came through the gate and stood with me on the other side. He asked me how I felt and what was going on. We talked about how I was regarding leadership as less about what I was doing, the steps I was willing to take and how much I was giving it away to the "other", waiting (yes, again) for them to let me know when to take the next step. I noticed that I dismissed the "solution" that had been there immediately as soon as I started to let intellect and logic take charge – something in me already "knew", I just wasn't prepared to listen or trust myself.

I finally began to see that I had now achieved the task – of leading the horses through the gate. It wasn't about them it was about me.

It wasn't about if they came, it was about if I went. And in order to go I had to let go of them, really let go, and not in some manipulative, pretend way.

I realized that this thing we bandy around as "leadership" is not some fine feeling of success, with everybody cheering you on. Leadership is the lonely walk down the field, leaving the comfort of everyone and everything behind and wondering if what you are doing is the right thing, even when it makes no sense to you at the time. The last thing it is is comfortable. And no one is cheering, at least I didn't hear them.

Then one of the miracles that I have come to experience with horses began to happen. As Mark and I had been talking the horses had been slowly, but surely, grazing their way down towards the gate. They were no further than a couple of metres away now. How weird was this?! I had let go completely of their doing anything in any direction of any gate – and here they were!

Mark commented, "Funny isn't it – they can't get through now, even if you wanted them to." I had shut the gate. I had shut the gate! Another light bulb went off in my head. I do that, shut gates. If people don't come, when and where I want them to, I shut the gate, they've had their chance, they are obviously not interested, and that's that, *finito*, all over! I don't usually leave gates open for people or horses to come as and when they are ready to come, in their own time and in their own way.

I opened the gate and in minutes both horses walked calmly, happily through the gate and followed us up the lane to the ménage.

The insights and understandings were tumbling over one another. I needed to trust myself. I needed to take the lonely walk. If I didn't go – what was there to follow, some vague idea? I had to take the first step. Then I needed to leave the gate open, so that whoever or whatever I was "leading" could go through the gate when it was right for them to do so. Leadership was about me, not about what anybody else did, that was up to them. And there was a sense of freedom right there.

In an hour or so I had been able to learn some lessons that some people never learn in their whole lives. The power of this learning was that it was real, a fully emotionally embodied experience that will remain with me for the rest of my life. My world was changing, yet again. But that was only part one of my day.

We had some lunch and then went out to do some more work in the round pen.

When I say pen, I mean a number of white sticks in the ground with tape linking then together to create the impression of a barrier. The pen was about 30 feet in diameter. I was working with Maddie.

My task on this occasion was to have her walk around me in a circle, with me standing in the middle, her walking around the outside. I had a short rope that I could use like an extension of my arm, but I was not allowed to touch her with it.

Off we went. I mean off *I* went. *She* didn't go anywhere. She stood on the edge of the circle, her head lowered, her eyes almost closed.

I stood in the centre, my back rigid, shouting at her "Maddie, Maddie, come on! Let's go! Walk on! (horse terminology)", doing my sergeant major impersonation. Well, that had no impact at all. It didn't entirely feel right to me, so god knows what she thought about it.

I wasn't very comfortable about having the rope in my hand so consequently it just hung there. Isn't it funny how sometimes we have resources at our disposal and we never use them? We are almost frightened of using them.

I kept trying and trying and getting nowhere, redoubling my efforts at the same thing (that wasn't working!). That's always a good strategy – try harder at what isn't working in the first place! Mark said, "That doesn't seem to be working." Great.

So I stopped what I was doing for a moment and gathered myself together for one last shot at this. I was at the point of giving up, but I was going to give it one last go, really go for it, and really make it happen. I took a deep breath, filling my whole body. I focused my whole being on Maddie, and on her moving. I felt strength and energy flow through my body. I used my voice, my arms, I swirled the rope. I was positive, but not demanding. Then in one moment I literally felt a rush of energy come out from the centre of my stomach and go towards Maddie. AND SHE MOVED. And she walked around me in a circle. Another miracle! I had just moved a half ton of horse that was half asleep with the power of my own mind, energy, belief, whatever you wanted to call it! I don't care. I know what I experienced.

I did not know it then, but that moment was to change my life and that of many other people. That was the moment I was later to describe as a moment of absolute Unstoppability. In that moment there was faith, belief, trust, courage, energy, alignment. It was the living, energetic moment and I had just gone there.

Thursday 6 September 2001

I am in a funny space at the moment. I am enjoying work, enjoying my achievement in my Masters, considering the doctorate. I have a renewed energy towards my horse-riding.

I feel an emerging life-force in me, something about me that I am coming to realize and need to release – this business of waiting for the other to signal connection. Not taking my own responsibility. And when I did, the other disappeared. In the ring, when I had clarity, Mark disappeared. Clear with myself, uninterrupted by what I thought others might think. That happened in my Masters too, those last few weeks when I was focused on my intention.

So only when I am clear with myself can I truly move forward with focus, unencumbered by anything or anyone else – and then just be.

Then this concept of aligning my body's energy behind my thoughts – the energy of my whole being, the full force of my personality. I think that this is what is called charisma, the alignment of one's intention, energy and focus – complete congruence in the expression of self. This is attractive and what is seen as leadership. It is compelling and hypnotic, irresistible, in whatever form you see or hear it. It reaches into the soul and stirs a distant memory; it is instinctive, it is natural leadership.

I am responsible and I must take leadership responsibility for myself, and myself alone, and not worry about who is following. That's not the point. And it means me looking back not forward.

"Trust". This is a word that I have trouble with. I think there are very few people whom I trust, and sometimes in not trusting myself I am not able to trust others.

"Respect" is changing. Love and dominance in the horse world. Dominance, trust, love all come together, but through the presence and force and congruence of one's personality.

"Courage" I said. When did I say that? In the ménage.

"What do I need?" Mark said.

"Courage" I said. Courage and belief that I can do this. I questioned courage. Why do I need courage, if there is congruence and focus – unless there isn't?

Sunday 9 September 2001

What keeps coming back is that moment of alignment – intention, clarity, belief, focus, energy, choice. I took responsibility but it felt like freedom. It felt open. My energy went out to the horse and she moved. In that place I didn't need courage, because I had truth.

Truth is pure. An alignment of thought and energy. It is something beyond words. A feeling. You feel it in special moments.

Trust – this is a word or a concept that is mostly about self, as is everything.

The purpose is to realize that I can take the freedom that is already there for me. Taking responsibility, being accountable – these are words often heard in the corporate arena – weighty and burdensome, promising of punishment – they create the opposite effect – taking true responsibility and personal accountability based upon belief and one's own purpose offers freedom. And I need to follow myself – the spiritual energy that is there within me and is trying to get out, like a moth flapping against the light-shade, not realizing that there is a way to get out and be free. It is not really trapped at all.

It is my choice. The clarity of my intent to myself. The impression of others is exactly that, their impression. No one can ever be inside my mind and experience what I experience as truth, so it is irrelevant what they think about my experience.

Courage is what you need, or think you need, when your actions are not aligned to your beliefs.

This is why I am ready to contemplate the next step I want to take, because while it may seem strange to others, to me it represents complete alignment.

My truth. Horses demand this of me, in a way never demanded by people. Because I am "good with people" I am able to intuit their signals and I operate on this level, double processing.

But horses are too quick for this. The double processing confuses the signals, the energies are not aligned.

They demand truth. They demand your truth. And in this truth there is joy, freedom, focus, being alive to the moment, beauty and my unique truth.

What I had experienced was very powerful. What was significant was not the events in and of themselves, it was my capacity to make sense of them in ways that could help me move forward in my life. You are not developed from the outside, only by what you do on the inside. It was about *my* capacity to learn.

Mark would say to me that I wasn't like other people, that I was special. I couldn't really see it myself, I almost couldn't accept this of myself, and I would dismiss it as flattery. He said to me that I needed to set myself some completely audacious goals – well that suited me down to the ground. He was talking my kind of language, and I had already begun.

That year I had recruited a new member for my team, his name was John.

Recruiting new learning and development people was always difficult, but it had to be done as one of my team had taken a promotion into another business. John turned up about half way through the recruitment process. I greeted him in the entrance of our building and took him up to the meeting room. A short while into the conversation the old hairs on the back of my neck started doing their thing. This was my man. He was talking my language and on a level I did not get to with most people in business. John was special. But this was just the first interview, and he had to get through the dreaded tests and a second interview with my boss.

In the end it came down to two people, one of them being John. Peter and I made the decision; it was to be John. He was on holiday somewhere in the Mediterranean, but we had his number, to let him know. We did. He and his wife had champagne.

We applied for references, as you do, and a funny thing happened. One of the board members of John's previous company telephoned us to tell us how special John was, how lucky we were to have him and to make sure we took care of him.

Like I said, John was special. And his arrival in my team changed everything.

Once John had got settled in the company, I wanted to see what he would make of the horses, so off we went to the countryside. Unlike me, John had no interest in or experience of horses, so that was going to be interesting. I went along with tape recorder and video camera in hand to see what I could capture, by way of trying to understand what was going on.

We were working in the ménage area with Serendipity. John spent some time talking about a work relationship that he wanted to figure out and move forward in some way. He felt that this person did not believe in him, and so he could not flow in the relationship, just be himself – it was holding him back. His task was to lead the horse around the arena, but with no ropes or tack of any kind. So off he went. He stroked the horse, talking to it, engaging with it and within a pretty short space of time Seren connected with him and began to walk side by side with him around the arena. Every time I see one of these beautiful creatures connect with a person, of their own free will, it almost makes me cry. As John walked around the arena Mark said; "Why don't you test the relationship?"

There was a little cross-pole set up as a jump. John and Seren headed for that. John hesitated, looked at Seren, and she stopped. He stopped. Minutes later he was laughing at his own insight. He was the one who had hesitated. He was the one who had doubted. He was the one who had stopped – not the other, not the horse. So here was the mirror, again, thought translated into action, translated into outcome.

And here was another person who had had this experience and could understand it from the inside, how it felt, and how only part of it could be expressed in language. So often, in life and in business, we imagine that change occurs very strikingly, suddenly – whole organizations are doing something different because a new process has been introduced. Or if we want to lose weight we expect to lose half a stone in a week. Change does happen quickly, but I have come to notice that it often happens one person at a time. Now there was another person in my business who had experienced the power of horses as a catalyst to transform. I didn't know it then, I dared not hope it then, but I was on my way.

It's funny, but as the idea begins to emerge from its chrysalis we tend almost to expect people to reject it and then we are surprised when they do. In one way why was I worried? What was so different in learning and development about using horses instead of ropes, boats and dead rabbits? But in my mind it was so fragile, so new, that someone might kill it before it even began. So I began talking about "the board this" and "the board that", like these 10 men were a homogenous group of people that thought and acted as one and the likelihood of them paying any attention to what I had to say about horses was one of those David Brentisms – "Are all the pigs watered and ready to fly?" But this was all in my mind, me inventing my own demons!

Friday 9 November 2001

There is no board. There is no organization. Only me and my responses – how I choose to see things… I am going to think differently about myself – to have a relationship with myself, respect myself, not put myself last – take care of myself. Think about managing my states more actively, be more future-orientated, draw a line over the past and go forward.

Focus, energy, alignment, acceptance. Dreaming, pictures, video – pictures everywhere I look. Find a coach that will take me to become a world-class rider.

At work we began debating an organizational change programme that would re-energize the leadership as part of what was now a global business, after some time of uncertainty. The stakes had been raised and a step change in leadership was needed. I knew that the time for the horses had come but how was I going to swing this? A small group had been set up by the Chief Executive Officer, Stewart, who I knew well and liked a great deal. This group was to lead the Organizational Transformation Programme. There were a number of other guys from the business, my boss and a consultant who had worked with the business for quite some years. We began to create a change programme, but somehow I was never able to connect the horses into the architecture – it felt too personal, like a hobby-horse, if you will pardon the pun.

It needed to become a more objective approach and, of course, no one had ever done this before! Businesses always want to be sure that some other huge named conglomerate has done something like this before and that everything would be OK.

I managed to engineer a couple of significant steps. I invited Phillip, a respected external coach and consultant to the business, and a couple of his colleagues to come and experience the horses for themselves – to get their professional, unbiased opinion, that would be respected and valued by Stewart and "the business". Phillip had been intrigued and knew that my experiences had been very powerful and that there must be something in this thing. He was very supportive in helping me move things forward. Dates were set for them to work with the horses, during December and January.

At this time Mark had connected with an old friend of his called Perry, meaning that there were more facilitators, enabling us to work with larger groups of people than just one or two. He was very anxious for Perry and I to meet, sure that we would get on.

Sunday 18 November 2001

I feel I am getting clearer and clearer all the time about who I am, what I stand for. Watching *Gladiator* the movie makes you think – what do you leave behind for your life, across the generations? In one sense I leave my mark in my children and their children and their children's children. I will be a dusty old photograph in an album, god knows where. Watching that film, a story from history, with all the differences that that brings, it's still about the same stories and struggles, the same human issues of power, love, trust, the stuff that goes on between us always.

What will my life have been about, a succession of jobs in big companies?

The outer shell?

Life has got to be about the inside stuff, not the outside. "That's just geography" as Julia Roberts remarked to Richard Gere in *Pretty Woman*.

Then came the tipping point.

A proposal for the transformational programme had been prepared. It was a good, sound, solid proposal that included much of our principles and approach, such as coaching and dialogue workshops for the top teams, but in another sense there wasn't anything strikingly new about it. I was to attend a short meeting with Stewart, the CEO, Peter, my boss, and John, to go over the proposal and give our views. Peter and I had a quick conversation before the meeting and I said once again that I really felt that in order to create a step change we needed to do something different, and that working with the horses would provide this… I was getting desperate as I could see this proposal being swept along without even an impression of a hoof-print on it. Peter didn't say "No", he just said "Don't mention the horses yet, it's not the right time."

I went into the meeting, biting my tongue one more time. But I hadn't reckoned on John. Neither had Peter.

The pleasantries over, Stewart asked, in his CEO kind of way, whether this was going to do it for us. There was a gap, a hesitation, a breath. John had the paper in his hand. He slapped it down on the desk and said, "If you want breakthrough this isn't it. This is just like any other change proposal I have ever seen!"

I stared at John, my mouth hit the floor. I thought – Oh no, what is he saying? Is he mad? Suicidal? What did I bring him for?

Stewart looked at Peter. Peter looked at me. I looked at John.

Stewart said, "What do you mean? I thought we had the best people working on this? If we don't do this, what are we going to do? What other ideas have you got?" There was my life-line. I hesitated. I looked at Peter and thought, I know what we said but it's now or never.

"Well," I said, regaining my composure, "we do have some different ideas, as a matter of fact… that we believe will produce the step change we are seeking. And it's basically working on leadership development using horses rather than ropes, rafts and dead rabbits!

When you have to connect with an animal without ropes or restraints of any kind, and have that animal accept you as the leader, you have to go to a completely new paradigm of leadership. You have to take responsibility for leading yourself, and only then will the horse choose to follow you."

John joined in and offered his own experience with Seren and how it had given him a new insight into his leadership approach.

Stewart was doing really well by now, you'd think people could suggest this kind of thing to him every day of the week and he wouldn't bat an eyelid. I didn't discover until the next day that he felt in a state of shock.

We said that Phillip and his colleagues were going to work with the horses to "test out" the approach and that we would take their feedback, but that we felt that we had something here that could provide the business with a real catalyst for change in the senior leadership group.

And so we left the meeting. The idea had been articulated and Stewart had not said "No" – I took that as a "Yes", and my confidence began to grow.

This was becoming a reality. Had it not been for John, and what he said in that moment, his complete authenticity in pretty much always telling you exactly what he thinks about anything, this story would not be what it is.

The universe continued to bring forward people and opportunities.

That same week I had a meeting with one of the key players in the business. Ironically, it was Tim – the guy who had offered me my "waiting" insight.

We had had a few meetings and he was very interested in leadership and learning. He wanted to do "something" with his team towards the end of January and did I have any ideas?

DID I HAVE ANY IDEAS?! We talked for about an hour, discussing what he wanted to achieve through a workshop of a couple of days, how he would like the team to feel, think and be as they faced a new business challenge.

I said that we could do something experiential and to leave it with me. I would come up with something! As we completed our conversation and left the restaurant he asked me, "What are we going to be doing, then?"

Over my shoulder I replied, "Oh, we're going to do something with horses, but just leave that to me" just like it was the most natural thing in the world. I then got out of there before he could say anything else or change his mind.

A pilot workshop had just been born in my head! I had people! I had dates! This was real! And it was only six weeks away.

Wednesday 2 January 2002

And so a new year begins. I am in my 39th year, on the threshold of the next phase of my life. My head swims with all my thoughts and plans. I am reading like a maniac and planning and connecting. I am "listening" to myself a lot more, paying attention and just listening – and it's definitely paying off.

I am helping people at work, definitely impacting, changing their lives... and I have the ability to inspire... inherently... so what could I achieve if I put my mind to it?

I am using myself differently.

Over these next two years I will complete my doctorate, my journey into leadership; build my knowledge, my speaking and writing capability, using all the techniques at my disposal.

Now that we were doing a workshop, we needed to design one.

A design day was arranged involving myself, John, Mark, one of Phillip's colleagues, Nic, and Elaine, who worked with Mark and Perry, whom I had not yet met.

We spent a day creating the workshop design that we would use for Tim's team at the end of the month.

Mark had been approached by a German news company and had done a feature with them. He had asked me to "do a piece to camera" for the feature, as they say in the media, on using horses in personal development.

Wednesday 9 January 2002

It felt like one of those pivotal days today. Saw myself on the video talking about the horse. And I could not deny it, I was mesmerizing, I was like a shining light. I amazed myself! I felt like the ugly ducking looking at its reflection in the water and seeing a swan gazing back at it. Where were all those words coming from?

And later, in the meeting, I had some insight about Mark, which I delivered with my usual aplomb – and there was a moment of complete silence. And Perry said from his heart, "What an eloquent lady you are. You just silenced us all with your eloquence!" And we all just looked at each other – because I had! This is what I have. I am starting to see it, feel it, know it.

John is so amazing – what a find. He is truly outstanding; he is just so grounded and humble in many ways, he only has an ego when he remembers to have one.

I have such a sense of my own light, my emerging possibilities.

LESSONS I HAVE LEARNED

The only person that I can lead is myself. Whether people choose to follow is completely up to them. If I do not have the faith and belief in where I am going, then no one will follow me. They do not follow me anyway; they are following something in themselves – an echo, a reflection that only appears to be in me, that they do not yet understand.

Hire people that make the hairs on the back of your neck stand up.

Leadership territory involves doing things that have never been done before – that takes faith, belief and trust – in yourself. You cannot wait for someone else to give you this. You have to go first. The lonely walk.

The moment of fear, the moment of doubt, is when leadership is required – and no one is cheering. Very often you are on your own – big time. They will congratulate you years after the event. And by then it won't matter anyway!

Getting close to your heart's desire, your dream, your purpose, whatever you want to call it, begins to unleash a level of energy, an emotional, mesmerizing, captivating communication of your whole being – words line themselves up in a whole new way. This degree of congruence and alignment is very difficult to stop. It's sometimes called inspiration.

PRINCIPLES TO LIVE BY

The truth is always there, not an absolute truth on the outside but your truth on the inside. It is a guiding light.

Lead yourself alone, and don't worry about the others.

Connecting to your heart's desire will release a new level of energy in your life.

EXPANDING YOUR CAPACITY TO LEARN...

Now that you have a sense of your goals and your values the direction is set. The next stage is action. Making it happen, living the future one moment at a time. This may be where you will call upon your belief, your faith, your confidence in yourself.

The better you feel about yourself, the more positive you feel, the greater your ability to take small risks, to begin the journey.

Make a list in your journal of all the things you love to do that make you feel great. Plan them into your life – daily, weekly, monthly, annually – whatever.

Make a list of people that you love to be with, people who support you, love you, never judge or criticize you.

Make sure you are spending lots of your time with these people.

If you admire something about someone, tell them, give it to them.

You may think they already know – they won't. And watch as the positive energy comes back to you, from somewhere else – somewhere unexpected.

Avoid people who do not make you feel good.

Sort out some music that just makes you feel like you could take on the world – fighting music – the sort that you sing along with in the car. Use it to make you feel invincible, unstoppable.

Look at the clothes you are wearing. When you go out to face the world do you feel, when you look in the mirror, that Jim Carey "somebody stop me!" kind of a feeling? If not, have a clear-out, find some stuff that begins to express who you are going to be, not who you have been.

Develop attitude.

Make a list of positive affirmations about yourself – as many as you like – at least 20. Say them out loud. This increases their power because you are using more layers of energy.

Whatever your goals, find someone (or, even better, two or three people) who you can tell, who will support you – and not roll around the floor laughing. Speaking them out loud starts to allow the universe to re-organize itself. And you can be sure that someone will know someone who will be able to help you.

If you are able to, go on a course of some kind, or read some books on an area of interest to you, or on self-development or growth – go for it. But remember, process, process and process in your journal.

Recognize every small step you are taking as a positive change. Be amazed by it.

Talk about it. Write about it. And look back in your journal and notice that your life is changing. Write about that.

6

Uncharted Territory

Where are you going?

Now, there's a thought. If you do know, did you decide? Or did someone else, someone in your past or present? Is it somewhere you are *supposed* to be going? Is it real? Does it make you feel alive?

When you move into the living moment you suddenly realize that there aren't any maps of how things are supposed to be. You are really on your own, with only yourself to depend upon and you get to be in charge as well, you get to be worthy, to be valued, to be enough, you get to lead. And often you think it's about the horse, and it's not. It's about you. Everything is *about* you. There has never been another one of you in the whole of time and there will never be another you in the whole of time – the only thing you can do is be who you are and fit into the world in the way that only *you* can. As contemporary poet and consultant David Whyte says, "The universe is holding its breath for you to take you place... the unique place in all of creation that only you can fill". You take the journey with the horse and all the time, every moment, the mirror is there – how often do you look and what do you see? Because you see, it's not a one time intellectual understanding, it's an ongoing conversation with the world.

FINDING MY PLACE

Things had moved so quickly. Here I was preparing to co-facilitate a workshop for Tim's team using horses in leadership development.

I mean, how had this happened? I couldn't believe it.

I was beginning to understand leadership in a completely new way. Not only was I understanding it, I was living it. And it was working. I was using my energy, my belief and my alignment to truly "lead" myself and somehow trust that stuff would happen, and it did. The other thing was, it didn't *take* energy, it *gave* me energy. It wasn't about doing, it was about being, and being who I already was – the eternal paradox, the easiest and hardest thing in the world, just to be who we are.

I was also beginning to understand why I wanted so passionately to do this kind of work. Why I needed to do this kind of work. I had to do it for my own journey of self-discovery, but I also had to help others to find their own freedom. I had begun to read David Whyte and he so beautifully articulated the struggles in the modern workplace. He helped me feel that I was on the right track here.

And so, on a cold morning in January, in a huge indoor arena in Stow on the Wold, we began.

The overall design of the two-day workshop was an interplay of facilitator input, group dialogue in the conference room and interaction with the horses in the large indoor arena.

The purpose of the first session was to engage the team in thinking about how they might be holding themselves back, how they might be settling for their "comfort zone", which when you examine it closely isn't comfortable at all, it's just familiar.

After coffee, at around 11.00am, it was time to go and join the real facilitators – our four legged friends. There was a lovely moment when we all walked out into this vast space, and from the corner of the arena two dark brown horses emerged inquisitively into the space, their coats contrasting sharply with the sandy arena. The air was heavy with expectancy and anticipation. Little did the delegates know that we were as much on the edge as they were. This was not the safety of a carefully planned PowerPoint presentation with hand-outs – this was the edge of life.

We worked with a couple of exercises, just as I had done in my sessions with Mark. And the group began to enter that most terrible of territories, where the old paradigms, upon which their leadership of control was founded, begin to wobble, but as yet they had nothing else to put in their place.

The horses also take you into the space where you begin to see the futility of your words alone, unless they are backed up by fully embodied actions, and that takes self-belief. And on the edge of everything you know it is tough to create the self-belief that you need to stand on the edge, never mind go over it!

We reached lunchtime, where everyone was beginning to think that this had been a fine idea in theory, but now they were not so sure – discomfort, confusion, frustration is not that much fun on your own, but when you have to go through it in front of your team-mates it borders on the unpleasant!

After lunch, further exercises allowed the individuals to explore some of the ways in which they were holding themselves back, and as we went to work with the horses again we were looking for breakthrough.

During the afternoon each person achieved a breakthrough in their work with the horse – anything from the horse moving around them in a circle on a long line to putting on a bridle to "join-up", where the horse followed them around the arena, without the need for any ropes or bridles. Each time an individual had a moment of breakthrough they had to make an internal shift in their thought pattern, their belief structure about themselves that they were mirroring onto the creature in front of them… "It doesn't like me", "I'm just not doing this right", "I don't have the technique yet".

They produced a positive affirmation, a verbalization of the new thought as an access point for change.

By the end of the day we had all travelled a long way, but there was still some way to go. There had been a moment of "storming", as often occurs in group facilitation, and you could feel the tension in the air. Such a lot was going on in so many different layers it was impossible to sense or absorb it all on the verbal level.

The next day our theme was for "Team Stretch" – what did this team really want for itself, as individuals and as a group?

They had an opportunity to think about their goals and dreams over the next five to 10 years, what did they really want – and underneath these goals, what did they really represent? What were the experiences and values that were crying out to be lived?

The group worked in pairs, coaching each other as they each uncovered the layers of what they really wanted in their lives and the silent appreciation of the gap between how they were living their lives (and what this was costing) and how they wanted to live their lives. Through a process of visualization they each took a journey into the future and experienced the goals, and realized that they had discovered what they truly wanted. The emotion started to bubble up, the energy began to be released.

After lunch we prepared to go out to the horses again. We stood in a circle and chanted our affirmations whilst stirring music increased in its intensity as our voices rose. There's no doubt about it, it was a bit strange, but it did do something to the energy in the group.

Out with the horses we took things to yet another level. Each individual, one after another, connected with one of the horses. Each team member was running around the arena, with a horse trotting along beside them. They were leading themselves and consequently leading the horses. They were supporting each other and witnessing the stretch in every person. They had found something in themselves that the horses could connect to, that they could connect to. It was magical.

I recorded my experiences and feelings in a little notebook throughout the two days; some of the things I wrote:

I see individuals truly sharing their feelings about one another – building relationships with themselves and each other – power, energy, developing their comfort in a new relationship space. Emotion is present in the room.

I am touched as I am experiencing the hearts, needs, minds and souls that I have sensed within the scope of my energy field – and I can feel it! Support, strength, skill, unity, its effect on everyone else. There are many voices, no one voice more powerful than the rest. A powerful place, a supportive place. Any situation comes down to love. I can be the whole me.

By mid-afternoon on the second day I was feeling the energy in the room so intensely that my teeth were chattering and I was visibly shaking, trembling. Because the changes that were occurring in these individuals were on the emotional and energetic level, not on the rational and logical level, many of the changes were beyond the scope of language and could only be hinted at, but they were palpable in the room.

The final exercise was one of acknowledgement. Expressing the wonder you had seen in another and what it meant to you.

To stand face to face with someone, who is telling you something that they see and value in you, is one of the most terrifying places for a British executive to go… The last vestiges of holding ourselves together fell away, and as even more emotion was released the air became electric.

The group made some final comments on a feedback form and we all left that magical place, heading back to our worlds that would never be the same again…

In those two days I encountered something I had never truly known in my life before, and I glimpsed it for an instant. For a moment I mistook it for something else, and for a long time did not acknowledge that I was the source of my own experience, tapping into something stronger than me. I had hinted at it in my notebook when I had written, *this is all about love*. I did not know where those words had come from. They just came out of a stream of consciousness. I did not realize their significance for many, many months.

I wrote in my dairy that night…

Wednesday 23 January 2002

Well, I made it happen, the most amazing workshop anyone has ever seen. It was almost too much to bear. Was it all that, the horses or something else – or was it all connected? And that's why I felt what I felt.

When we went into the final exercise it blew all my electromagnetic circuitry out of the water! Mark, Tim, Harvey, John, Nic, Alan – what came back to me was me, the essence of all of me and how I had allowed them to be them – it was amazing. I cried throughout the whole thing and, as I didn't know this was going to happen, did not have my waterproof mascara – nightmare.

I talked to Tim a few days later. Tim said that he had changed, he was more confident and felt he knew how to help his team – he was aware of his leadership (his affirmation).

Then came the feedback forms through the fax machine at home. Disbelief and wonderment as each one came through. Words that came from the depths of each individual – insights and personal discoveries:

Knowing myself for the first time in 50 years.

Nothing seems out of reach. Aim for the edge, then the next and the next.

Leadership is key for our business and all leaders need to embrace the concept of the "self".

I just thought this was a unique experience and was absolutely brilliant.

Of course, there were things that people struggled with, but in essence it was pure magic and it delivered real breakthrough in two days!

For Mark, who had been working with equine-based coaching for a number of years, it was a long held dream come true; for me a dawning realization of what it really means to hold a space for someone, to enable them to transform themselves; for John, Nic, Elaine and Perry, a joy in real human growth. The experience we had created and lived through had created a bond and closeness, a sense of possibility, an invincibility that was as solid as a rock. Well, that's what it felt like at the time. But there were hairline cracks that I just didn't want to see and so did not allow on to my radar screen. I was pursuing my vision and I was determined that nothing would stop me.

Throughout the course of my Masters degree I had become interested in NLP (Neuro Linguistic Programming). I don't say studies because they weren't studies in that I was studying someone else's model – I was delving into my own question, which was much more fun! I had always been rather sceptical about NLP as those who got involved in it always seemed to become over-zealous – almost like they had been brainwashed! But over the course of the last 18 months several people that I knew and thought were fairly even keel types began telling me stories of how it was helping them change their lives. So my curiosity was piqued.

My first expedition into the world of NLP was a bit of a baptism of fire. A good friend had begun working with Paul McKenna and Michael Breen, renowned experts in NLP training. She invited me along to an afternoon session, saying that I just had to see this stuff in action. I had known her for many years as someone who always operated on the edge, so there was usually something to be learned.

The day I went along Dr Richard Bandler, the co-founder of NLP, was running one of the sessions, so I jumped at the chance.

I sat at the back of this huge room, with about 350 people in it, watching and listening to this weird guy at the front of the room, who had not seen a hairdresser for an age and had the loudest Hawaiian shirt I had ever seen outside of a holiday resort. As I sat there, listening to him swearing and telling stories, never finishing them, frustration began to set in and I wondered when he was going to get to the point and inform me of something that would be of any use. Then I began to get this funny sensation. I started to relax in my seat, the room went kind of fuzzy and I was looking down this sort of tunnel, all the while beginning to float.

Now you have to understand that the people there were on a two-week course – I had gate crashed, by invitation of course, for two hours, but here I was experiencing what I later discovered to be my first induced trance.

I did not realize the genius of the man until many months later. But this is often what learning is like – when you first encounter it, it seems to be the weirdest experience, it is only when you delve into it and wrestle with it that it comes to make sense.

Anyway, I wanted to know more and arranged to have some one-to-one sessions followed by a short course with a small number of delegates with Centre NLP based in Leicestershire. It was certainly fascinating stuff and I began to read everything I could on this new performance psychology.

In late 2001 I set up an internal NLP programme in the business, with a follow-up in February 2002.

As I got into NLP, I loved it. It was like discovering a whole new world and it was certainly challenging everything I knew about learning and change.

On the February programme we worked with goals, dreams, time-lines and beliefs. We talked about the things we wanted to achieve over the next five to 10 years, what those experiences would be like. We worked with each other on some of the beliefs we needed to challenge about ourselves if those dreams were to become a reality. This workshop was a life-changing experience for me. It helped me to crystallize what I wanted over the coming years; to turn my dreams into concrete plans that were completely real. I discovered that although I believed I had everything I needed to achieve everything I wanted, I actually did not believe that I *deserved* to have what I wanted, that I was somehow "*not worth it*".

Not worthy enough. That was a shocker! But as long as I believed this about myself, who would believe in me? So, what you do in NLP, faced with this situation, is – you change the belief, which is what I did. And I came to believe that I did deserve what it was that I wanted.

I set my goals along a "time-line" into the future and I physically walked into each experience and felt what it was like, who was there, what was happening – teaching my mind and body, what to seek out, what to pay attention to and to understand what each goal represented.

Because the goals we want to achieve in life are really about living the values that are critical to us, that are hard-wired into our neurology – it's never really about the goals, it's about the experience, the feelings and the emotions.

At this workshop I determined that I would have my horse before I was 40, and of course not any old horse, but a Spanish stallion!

I would become a leader, a commentator on life, love and leadership in the modern corporation. I had something to say and it would be said. I would create a happy home for my family, represented by the kitchen table overlooking horses in the fields, with the girls coming in after school. My home and my work would all be in the same place and I would not spend hours of wasted time on endless motorways. I would become a speaker, a commentator, a recognized expert on leadership and learning. I would be on the front cover of *Harvard Business Review* in 10 years!

As I worked with my goals I noticed how I shied away from asking or articulating what I truly wanted. At first, I asked for what I believed might just be possible from here, from now. You know, "realistic, achievable" etc. I hesitated to speak my heart's desire, because I might not be worthy of it – I was censoring myself before anyone else could have a chance to lie on the floor holding their bellies in laughter! (Funny thing is, when you utter your heart's desire the last thing people do is laugh.) Denying my possibility, not realizing that whatever was my deepest desire was completely available to me if my dream was congruent, aligned, true and for the growth of myself and others.

I mean, who was I to ask for such things – and on the other hand, why not? Somebody has to do it, why not me?

I did not know it then but the course was now set. I just had to sail the ship.

Now the thing about sailing ships is that you have to put them in the water, you have to put the sails up and go with the wind.

I realized that as I began to speak my dreams out loud they began to become more real. And each time I spoke them to someone new, I accessed a unique state of positive energy – I felt fantastic. And the funny thing was, it was infectious. I would go higher and higher, and the other person would start to shift as well. Other people began to become engaged in my dreams; the energy began to spread.

After the first workshop we ran I was driving along thinking about my guru plan and thinking that I should get onto the conference circuit again. I used to do this quite a lot when I worked in American themed restaurants, but had not done much since the children had come on the scene. As I was considering how and where I could get into doing conferences again, a bolt of lightening struck from I don't know where. It said – why don't you invent the conference? Do your own – all about learning and leadership, a new paradigm including NLP, drama, poetry, horse work, body work – all this stuff I was discovering. If I didn't do it, then most business people would not come across it for about 25 years!

I called John immediately to tell him of my idea, to make it real. He thought it was fantastic. Of course, me being me, this wasn't to be any small affair but the largest conference on leadership ever held in the world! I was always a big picture sort of girl! And so the idea of "The Spirit of Natural Leadership" conference was born.

As my idea began to take hold other possibilities whispered in my ears. I was talking to John the following week about the work we were doing, not just with the horses but with our approach to learning and leadership in general, and as we were talking I suddenly realized that I wanted to set up a foundation of a kind, to create a space in this busy world where people could be who they were, who they wanted to be, who they were destined to be, where they could have time to connect with themselves and others, to learn and build relationships, to find new possibilities in their lives.

An oasis of humanity in the midst of the technological 21st century. It was like I realized this and it realized me, at the same time. As I spoke it, there was no turning back. An idea with such energetic alignment behind and in front of it would not be put down. John said, "The Centre for Natural Leadership". My destiny had just arrived, and I knew it.

A few days later I bought the company name and the web address. I had no intentions of doing anything at that time – but I thought that I'd be really cross if I set up the company three years later only to discover that someone else had bought the name.

Despite the workshop being such a success, I still had to stay focused on taking things forward – there were no fat ladies singing yet! John managed to secure the Marketing Director and his team as the next group. Their workshop would take place in March.

I attended a board meeting to present the "Step Change Leadership" strategy, including a leadership development workshop that involved working with horses. I have to admit, I was amazing that day, just for a few moments – I said that we would be working with intact teams and gave them the old "instead of ropes, rafts and dead rabbits" speech. I wish I'd had a camera when the Marketing Director leaned into the table and said, "Excuse me, Alison. Did you say horses?" suddenly realizing what John had talked him into. It was just beautiful.

I was able to say we had done a pilot, which had been very successful. Stewart had spoken to one of the participants and was "selling" the programme from the other end of the table, supported by my boss Peter.

I just sat back and watched! Then, at just the right moment, I produced a series of dates on a flipchart and asked them to let me know when they and their teams would be able to attend the workshops. By the time I walked out of the meeting, I had pretty much all the dates filled, not quite knowing how I had done it.

I looked forward to the next workshop, coming up in March, wondering whether we could possibly do it again. Had it just been a fluke, just that particular team?

I headed off to Stow again, eagerly anticipating the two days ahead, excited to be working with the team again, and hoping against hope that the magic would happen again. It did.

As once again the evaluation forms came over the fax machine, Steve looked at me quizzically across the toast and cereal and said, "What exactly are you doing with these people?"

Realizing that putting relationships first is a) what I want and b) the best way.

Realizing that you have to lead yourself before you can lead others.

Incredible – mere words can't explain – I feel it has enlightened me, both personally and professionally.

A greater sense of confidence and self-belief.

Allowed me to realize how I can release my potential in work and in life.

I had been involved in some pretty leading edge training programmes in my career, but nothing like this, these are not the words you see on training evaluation forms and yet it's what an industry strives to create! None of us could quite believe it.

But amidst the joy and elation there was something else.

My doctorate was entitled, "Creating the Conditions for Transformational Learning – Human Leadership Development through Equine-based Coaching". I wanted to figure this thing out, so I was expanding my level of awareness about what was going on – it was like my radar could pick up the most sensitive of signals.

I had decided to do my doctorate in this area because it represented integration for me – people, organizations, learning, leadership and horses – everything that I was passionate about.

But, as is often the case when like-minded people are drawn together, banded together in a common belief, any differences are at first ignored, then tolerated, before they begin to emerge into the open.

There were tensions emerging in the facilitation team, and I ignored them, hoping they would figure themselves out, just go away, just disappear; but these things never do, do they?

Wednesday 3 April 2002

I am having some doubts about Mark – some of the old stuff is still there – as was evident. My agenda is more open than Mark's agenda; they are not one and the same. They meet, but they are not the same…

I have to be true to me in the moment and know that that is all I can be – and that will be enough, more than enough.

Do people have these profound insights and then let them go, let them float to the bottom of the lake once more – and then blame the "stickability" of the process?

Abdicate reflection and responsibility. Everything that comes out our mouths is our world, we betray ourselves with our words. We construct our worlds in the words we utter.

The next team to come through was the HR team, the team of which I was a member. We wrangled and debated over whether I should go through the workshop as a delegate or a facilitator. Eventually, I thought – I will decide the role I will play, not anyone else! And I needed to be the organizational balance to the whole experience. I was the one who had to ground it back into the business.

So, some weeks later, I headed off to Stow once more.

Peter, my boss, was to be on this workshop. To say that Peter was a pragmatist was an understatement, so I wondered what he would make of it.

Somehow I was more involved this time. These people knew me well. Many of them had been on my journey with me. Some of the responses to the workshops were starting to move around the business now. The word was on the street. There were 14 delegates on this workshop, so I was also going to be facilitating the actual coaching with the horses as well as some of the work in the room. This was a new edge for me. But somehow we did it again!

Seeing my hesitancy in action. Recognizing the need to set things up for success and get out of the way.

Overcome my discomfort around horses. Feel comfortable opening up to others more. Learnt loads about myself and leadership.

Building relationships with beautiful, intelligent horses! I've shown myself that I am a bright person who can do things even more! Understanding the power I have and how I can use this in an effortless way.

Excellent – life changing, if I choose to make it so.

My boss wrote:

Exceptional – I came with high expectations and they were exceeded.

Friday 19 April 2002

Another amazing two days, an amazing week really. Insights crowd my mind – too many to bear. I don't know what's real.

My affirmation changed in the middle of saying it, in the middle of the workshop. Beyond thought – it just changed! It changed from "I am powerful beyond measure" to "I am loving beyond measure".

John and I saw that as you become your affirmation you go beyond it, you absorb it into yourself and you move on. This is what happened to me today in an instant…

What is this? I have no idea – this journey I am on. I am being carried forward on a wave and yet I can see how in one way healing is happening all around me. Everyone I touch – they grow, they expand, they feel compassion, acceptance and understanding – their very lives are being changed – and I am only just beginning to accept this.

> Lizzie once said to me that when we'd be out walking she'd notice that people would look at me – and she always wondered why.
>
> Someone described me as a beacon today – a beacon of light, powerful, inspirational, amazing, compassionate, caring…
>
> This has always been there, I am only now choosing to see it.
>
> I had the idea about my book. It is going to be about this story, the story of my life, an ordinary life.
>
> Someone's life changed today – it was amazing to watch – all our lives changed, took another turn as the rest of the world moved on by…

A week later we were back with the Manufacturing team. I thought that this was going to be the toughest workshop yet. These guys took no prisoners. Or rather they did take prisoners and didn't give them back!

It was a tough workshop. There was tension in the air, most of the way through the first day, but I had learned that this was often the pattern as the group entered confusion and the unsettling of its paradigms, the re-arrangement of its emotional and intellectual furnishings.

Even so, the positive affirmations came:

I am aligning myself.

I am letting go of my inhibitions.

I am confidently encouraging the team.

I am determined and succeeding.

All the time the words were attached to a resource state in each individual – it wasn't about the words *per se* – it was about what the words meant to each person, deep in their emotional layers. And as they accessed the words there was energy, there was a shift in their energetic, emotional and physiological state that was clearly visible. As they spoke the words they resonated in the air and achieved a different quality of connection with themselves, with the horse and the result.

On the morning of Day Two I wrote down what I was experiencing in the room as it was happening, as they were "checking in" – what they were thinking, what was going on for them:

The energy is different in the morning from the night before – confusion is in the air, resistance, which is manifest in quizzical looks and cynical humour. Authenticity pokes its head out now and again; there is movement in the group as one person wrestles.

My thought about the "expert" stage (in Torbert's model of leadership development) – I am holding that as a limiting expectation – although I have let go of it, in the speaking of it, it did not feel right as I said it.

Mark is reaching further inside than the stage of development, it is deeper than this, into the soul. It's a different developmental process.

I went riding this morning. Perry focused my awareness into my body – all the parts of it – and as I centred into myself I moved into a trance state of complete relaxation, my whole body relaxed with Rocky. Then he relaxed. I created trance in him.

Then when I tried to do too much – action rather than intent – it complicated things so much that we couldn't do it. But when I kept the state and used my energy and focus and intent – and whispered "trot" with my body – it happened effortlessly. My legs just dropped around him, just fell, no pushing, and I felt light in myself, at one with him, my whole seat relaxed into him. Everything disappeared as I went into trance.

Growth is a natural process.

I found myself doing so much less. There was so much energy in him ready to go. I was centred, relaxed, but could muster any amount of energy that we needed. Let go. Really easy – don't have to do anything, it was about being. Also letting go of all judgement of myself.

After the second session with the horses, each individual was sharing what they had learned over the two days of the workshop. Again the lessons were there for each individual – uniquely theirs, unique to their own personal world:

It's counter-productive to try too hard… the affirmation delivered for me.

The power of positive thinking, patience and focus, being with the horses, the euphoria it gave me inside. I learned about myself and the team.

Putting energy into rebuilding a relationship.

Look to the future, not to the past.

Goal visualization was extremely powerful, it surprised me what I saw and felt. It told me a lot. I am hooked on the feeling of the trot and looking forward. I couldn't believe it. The relationship and looking forward was really powerful. It will live with me forever.

And finally there was this one guy in the workshop who I thought had not been moved, had not achieved an insight. When he spoke I almost dropped my pen: "I saw something that I have not seen in a very long time; in 26 years, amongst all these training and skills courses, I realized that I had lost myself and in these couple of days I have found myself again."

Everyone in the room froze in the emotion and revelation in his voice. They froze in the moment from the energetic vibrations transmitted in his voice, they froze in the raw truth of it and they froze because he was the least likely person to say such a thing.

The evaluation sheets said it again:

Don't strain and try too hard. Trust my instincts.

Be confident in yourself; be focused, be patient; don't keep looking back, look forward.

I've identified a potential means of transforming my work-life balance by reducing the strain on me.

I feel a weight lifted off my shoulders and a re-establishment and reinforcing of my self-esteem, focus and confidence.

Turn the future into history!

The team did not, however, like one of the sessions in particular. This session involved the team members standing in a circle, with their eyes closed, chanting their affirmations to music that got louder and louder. None of the groups raved about this session, I mean, you have to admit that it is a bit weird, and I had my doubts about it, wanting to leave it out, particularly with some of the more "traditional" teams shall we say. But we kept it in as an element that began to build a new kind of energy before the second session with the horses.

It was interesting that, despite so much individual breakthrough, it was this session, with its weirdness and discomfort, which would often be talked about back in the world of the business.

I found it interesting that here we were trying to create innovation and creativity as a business, and people freaked if they had to stand in a circle with their eyes closed chanting some words over and over again (they were their own words after all) – I mean, no one was going to hurt them or anything! And if we couldn't do something so alien, so different, so new without rejecting it entirely, how on earth were we going to get to innovation – bit of a paradox?

Tuesday 30 April 2002

Another life-changing workshop and I am completely drained. This thing is really just incredible. The power of it – those who resist the most transform the most!

And being there, as part of the space, is a rare privilege. For me, it is love of a kind – and today my mother came to me, again and again – she was love and I am her and I am as much love as her. And I gave that out.

I never see myself as caring but actually I am deeply caring for others – I have never truly recognized this in myself, but it comes at me again and again… today driving back from Stow, listening to the music, I was overwhelmed with a sense of belonging, of finding my own space in the world, that was unique for me, that only I can fill. Tears ran down my cheeks.

I live in the twilight zone of the organization – the place of silent conversations, where the struggles of good and evil, courage and fear, beauty and love take place – the human stories, the hopes and lives of all the people searching for their place.

> I seek truth, but not the truth of absolutes, the truth that is love and light and a knowing of the soul. A recognition, a connection, an understanding, a compassion, a sharing, a healing.
>
> The eternal journey in the living moment.

Some months later I did a number of interviews with delegates who had participated in the workshops. As part of my thesis, I wanted to understand what the experience had meant to them and how it had affected their lives, inside and outside the organization. There were 22 interviews in total; below are a few examples of the kinds of insights and learning these trailblazers found for themselves.

GRAHAME

Grahame was a member of a functional executive group and led a team of managers himself. He felt about horses like I felt about walking around the top of the Empire State Building – terrified – so for him working with horses had an extra edge to it:

> *I think I had a real problem with horses, a fear of horses, beforehand so turning up and not knowing was better... when I got there, there was some panic.*

When the horses entered the arena he gravitated towards the centre of the group, keeping as many people between him and these creatures as he possibly could. As he remarked, he used the group almost like a shield.

During the initial exercises with the horses, being able to stand near a horse, on his own, touching and stroking it, was a major breakthrough for Grahame. He did not say a tremendous amount but there was a great deal going on inside for him. In a later interview, asked about the memorable experiences from the programme, he remarked:

> *The first thing would be to get this immovable object to run with me and stop when I stopped and then start immediately again, just asking it to – that was bizarre. I thought to myself – If I can get this animal to run with me I will be well pleased*

– and then it ran with me and I stopped, and it stopped. I was so excited I ran again and he ran again and without a doubt that was the major thing I have taken away from it in terms of a very personal sense of achievement.

But what was critical to Grahame was not that he had just run around an arena with a horse at liberty choosing to follow him, it was what that meant to his life:

This is what you can do if you really want to and are prepared to face whatever – this was probably more so for me than some of the others – what I could achieve if I faced up to this. I would never have dreamt of going near a horse so I would never have achieved it. There was also the idea of using the horse as an analogy for anything that I could do – that is the very transferable bit for me – at the end of the day, it was not just about horses.

Grahame reflected upon and used his experience with the horses to subtly change and enhance his leadership approach:

It was blindingly obvious to me at the end of Day Two that we can achieve masses of stuff if we get on and don't worry about things, just work our way through... I undoubtedly believe it has improved me as a leader, and my leadership repertoire, so I can choose many more different things now... there is complete mutual trust and I felt that very much with the horses eventually. I took those two days as not changing, more like becoming more of myself...

During the interview Grahame commented upon what he saw as the gap between how the team had been on the workshop and how they behaved when they returned to their real world, the insights and the learning seemed to slip away, little by little:

At the end of Day Two I was quite happy to run around with this horse and have it running and following me. I would probably have it run and stop, run, stop about four times which for me just illustrated what you could do, and it was about more than just work... what could we do if we could drop the shackles? Those horses didn't know me, and I didn't know them. To be honest, they probably didn't care very much for me, but you don't have to. You showed us what could be achieved – how our team could be open and honest, brutally open and honest. And yet I would say that every single person has come back into work and defaulted back to previous behaviour, it's almost like preservation mode, which just stifles what could be achieved. And I don't know how we move beyond that...

Grahame makes a pivotal point that touches any leadership development programme. Here was a man who met the possibility of great change in himself. But when we return to the home environment we meet the same patterns that we left behind. If we are to make real shift in our teams and networks we have to speak, act, do something different, be other than who we have been – the leadership, after all, is not about what we do in the arena with the horses at all – that is just a gateway – the real leadership challenge is when we move back into the relationship patterns that keep us, and everyone else, exactly where we are. Here there is no horse standing by saying "It's time to lead now", there is no encouraging coach whispering in your ear, "What else could you do?" You are alone, the moment passes – have you made a change or does the pattern pass on untouched and intact? This is the leadership question that we all face in organizational life.

JOHN

John was a senior leader within the business; a no-nonsense, practical sort of a guy – I know he won't mind me saying this – but the type of guy who had been in a few scrapes in his time and who could handle himself. To say he began with a touch of scepticism is a bit of an understatement:

I remember being sceptical and thinking to myself that I had better things to do, but then I thought – I am here so I may as well enjoy it... I had no idea.

He described his frustration at the first session with the horses, where the group was invited to lead the horses through some gates in the middle of the arena:

Tell us what we're supposed to do! There was no direction from the guys; now I realize that was deliberate.

As the programme continued and the group began to work individually with the horses:

I saw Jake lead a horse through the gates with a really positive attitude; I thought – If he can do it so can I. It all started to come together... that feeling of the horse running around after you, stopping, jogging – that gave me a lot of confidence. If you are in there with a bunch of negative people you are not going to get anything out of it. Every time I approached this horse from the side it ran away from me. It must have been sensing me as extremely aggressive. There's 20 other people here I can work with, why you?

What changed inside for John was:

A bit of belief in myself, which grew over the two days; I thought at the end of the two days that we could get the horses to juggle if we wanted! A realization that aggression isn't the way to get these animals to do what you want. It's understanding where they are – more intuitive than directional. You don't necessarily have to think about everything that you are doing – just go ahead, be calm and gentle and the horse follows. I was struck by the sense of calm that came over me.

What John was learning was pertinent to him, meant something to him, in his model of the world. It may not make absolute sense to us – but to him it is a deep understanding of another way to "use" himself.

John made several changes as a result of the workshop. He began to say "No" to more things, to prioritize, to delegate more to others. So how did his team respond?

My team say I am a lot calmer with them, a lot more easy going; they feel a lot more involved... I just feel I have an easier relationship with them, there's a lot more trust between them and myself. A lot more trust has helped me build that relationship – not so directional, now using the one-to-ones to sit down, take on their views, finding the direction for us together – much more open.

He described a meeting with a trade union representative that he had previously been regarding as difficult:

Before the session I would have been confrontational, because of frustration... but it was really nice because I did not have to say a lot... I was gently steering... I remarked to someone afterwards that I was like a little Buddha, I knew this was what we are going to get. I just kept calm and positive – I felt I almost willed it to happen. I did feel that was directly related to the course.

I am not one of those romantic people but I really feel I got something out of it – that inner calm, just concentrating on what you want to make it come true.

He realized in the interview that he had not been using some of the resources that he had developed in other meetings he had experienced recently. He realized that he had not revisited the goals he had created for himself, that represented what he really wanted in his life. He was incredulous with himself:

I need to start and take some of that time-out – I need to focus on what I want at work and tie that in to what I want at home.

Here again a critical point. We get so caught up in what we imagine everyone else needs and wants of us – "doing a good job" – it seems selfish to pause and consider, is this the job I want, am I doing it in the way that I believe in and where am I going with it?

And again, changing our behaviours does not occur in the arena, we are not "fixed" by something outside us. Even when we apply our learning once, it is not enough, we have to do it again and again, practise and experiment, reflect and do it again. This takes perseverance, determination, focus and attention. And you only get this if it really matters to you, personally, not just to the company's bottom line.

There is something else that is not visible in the words that you read here as quotes but something I commented upon in my own notes when I analysed this interview:

> *I am struck, listening to this interview, by the quality of the tone, the deep inquiry that is present, just pure inquiry into the life of an individual that seems to allow them to travel into new territory in the conversation. Matching of tone, pace, language. There is empathy and understanding for the story, experience, life of another. This is missing when only the words are considered – the space that is created here has a special quality to it, which is an inherent part of the process of openness. Also visible and audible here is the shift in the person in the midst of the interview. Renewed commitment, purpose and understanding.*

ELIZABETH

Elizabeth was an experienced leader who was fairly new to the team she was working with. A deep thinker, she quickly set the course in context for herself:

> *The journey across the two days was about me as a person, about who I am and where I am good and where I am not so good, about the things that limit me. It was the start of a process of recognizing what limits me, and it's actually nothing to do with anybody else, it's to do with what goes on in me, that's what limits me.*
>
> *I really got a kick out of working with the horses because it verified and validated what I suspected about myself, but I have never had the proof before. When I do people's performance reviews and ask them if there is anything I could do differently they all say "No, No, No", and I am thinking to myself that of course there is... so working with the horses and demonstrating that when I tied everything together that I knew I could do but found it hard to weave together – the clarity, the focus, the intention, and I think we called it energy – when those things come together there are gigantic steps as opposed to straightforward steps we can take.*

Elizabeth found the concept of offering people genuine compliments to be very powerful – not superficial compliments, but something "that says something about the individual and about their talents and their unique aspects, and that it's the uniqueness. It's pinpointing it as unique to that individual that actually makes the difference."

Elizabeth had to lead a new project in the business, one that she had been feeling ill-prepared to face:

I thought – Right, I am going to do this in a leadership kind of way, as in a hands on way – and it paid dividends I wouldn't have believed... it went off like a whippet out of the gate... for me it was about accepting that I was nervous and scared of making a real mess of a high profile activity, but then I realized that it was this thinking that was making me panic. And if I was thinking like this I was going to make a mistake, I was going to look a fool and it wouldn't be done.

I kept telling myself – Right, we are going to achieve this, there is no problem and we are going to get this done. We might not get it done through path A but we'll get it through Path A and Path B. That's how we will get there.

And we have achieved every milestone we have set. I think if I hadn't been in the programme I would have tried to do everything myself... it's not managing, it's leading, that's quite trite, but it's more exciting! It's about encouraging positive thinking; that's probably my biggest downfall – not believing in myself.

Elizabeth also realized that her life had swung out of balance recently, and that there were areas of her life that she was not attending to as much as she wanted – her family, her home, her friends and her health. A space to consider these in the context of her future gave her an opportunity to regroup. She is getting back to "my garden, my friends, the things that give me peace in my life".

The issues that hold us back in our lives are usually fairly deep in our structures and patterns, they are not the surface, moveable, cosmetic things – they are deeply personal and so require surfacing, which can be difficult. They require looking at by the individual, accepting in some way, and they require working with. This can feel "personal" or "not for business" as we can often feel these areas are separate, when in fact business is the person, and unless real change is generated in the person then the only change that can be generated in the business will be the mechanics.

What is also interesting here is that this level of change is difficult to describe. Sometimes what we feel or how we label something in our world does not fit anyone else. This doesn't matter because it is not about the word anyway, the word is not the feeling, it is a symbol or label of the feeling, and what is important is the feeling itself.

In her complimenting of others, Elizabeth was seeking the positive in others in a very authentic way, creating a positive frame for the relationship interchange, generating energy in them and in her. So simple, so effective, so enjoyable – so easy to forget.

ANNIE

Annie was the leader of a fairly large team and had been part of the business for a number of years. A practical person, she remained to be convinced about this idea of using horses for leadership:

When I received the invitation I was somewhat cynical, I don't know why I felt like that I just did. However, by the end of the first day I was converted and by the end of the workshop I went away with such a "wow factor" feeling that I completely changed my mind about the whole thing and saw just how interesting and beneficial the course really had been for me. Working with the horses was what was so powerful. On the first day when we tried to do things with the horses the feedback we got from them was clear. They didn't try to make you feel better; they told you exactly how it was. By Day Two you formed a connection with the horse so that they came with you and worked with you – I found that so amazing that I remember almost bursting into tears when I actually got the horse to walk through the cones – it was very real for me, that experience.

Annie learned to trust her own instincts, her own thoughts; trust what is right for her, believing in herself. She learned to keep trying, even when things weren't working, to keep moving, believing in herself again.
She describes joining up with Maddie:

About three times she just ignored me and kept walking away; I remember the moment where she seemed to click in. I just remember putting my head up close to her and saying something to her like, "Come on Maddie, let's do this together". I remember staying really close to her and just standing there, which probably seemed like a long time, consciously it seemed like a long time because you are quite aware of other people, but suddenly that all goes and you forget the other people and just go into what you are doing, you forget everything else, and that was to me the point at which it worked because I wasn't self-conscious. I stopped being self-conscious about what people were thinking... I was quite emotional about it and that's how I felt just after, even just talking about it; for me that shows how strong the experience was because I don't feel self-conscious about it at all now and it was an experience that I almost savour now because it was such a wonderful feeling; it's a bit like when I achieve that with my children or at work, you do feel that same kind of fantastic feeling, it's difficult to describe...

Annie was able to apply her learning with her children, describing the early morning flurry that so many of us know well, getting everyone out of the house on time, in the right clothes, fed, washed and brushed without having world war three every day. She found that she could connect with them more, just as she had done with the horse, leading them in a more effortless way, getting things done faster and easier; "Children will tell you as it is, so I am conscious of it when it works and when it doesn't work, and I know when I have completely ignored what I should be doing and it's quite interesting to see the results of that..."

Annie was learning to trust herself:

The need to trust your judgement has stuck with me again and again, so when I am dithering and then think to myself – Well this is what I believe – and then go with it, that is very powerful...

This learning for Annie could not have been prescribed from the outside, and could not have been predicted. Her learning is unique to her, as it is for everyone, depending upon their history and their own struggles. What is evident is her ability to take this experience, that remains so vivid for her, and use it again and again to help her with a current situation. She is actively using the resources she has developed for herself. In learning to listen and trust her own judgement, she is leading herself.

The individual stories go on and on. For each person there was a different lesson to learn, because they were at a different point, with a different struggle. Because the horse acts as a mirror, the only thing it can reflect is our own thoughts, beliefs, patterns and constructs.

LESSONS I HAVE LEARNED

I learned that I do not have to be speaking to communicate or to lead. I can "hold a space" for people and groups with my thoughts and my energy.

Every individual has their doubts and fears just like me, and all we see is the very tip of the iceberg.

People are amazing.

If I can think it I can live it, and it is invariably more than I could have ever imagined.

As I absorb and become my affirmation I transform, I move on from it and create another.

This space is where I belong.

PRINCIPLES TO LIVE BY

When there is emotion present there is energy present – real things are happening to people – more real than logic and intellect.

Do not run from emotion – your own or anyone else's. Embrace it. It is evidence of real change in action and it is an access to energy.

The only reason you are able to see anything in anyone else is because you have it within yourself.

FOR LIFE IN ORGANIZATIONS

Real relationships are not built just with time, they are built with authenticity and openness – the degree to which you reveal who you really are, not who you are pretending to be. Authenticity and openness cannot co-exist within a hierarchical power-based relationship. If your organization is seeking real step change, risk, innovation, it is going to require these kinds of relationships.

EXPANDING YOUR CAPACITY TO LEARN...

Think of the people that make up your life, think of each of them and the wonderful quality that you see in them. At an appropriate time, tell them this – the shining light you see in them, how they express it and why you are able to see it – how you also express this quality.

Everyone in your life is reflecting back a part of you – a unique relationship, a unique set of conversations and experiences that are a part of you both. This is why the death of a loved one is so terrible – because it can feel like a part of you has died too, especially when it is a parent – all that identity, all that history. But they also live on in you, a part of you, and you can bring them out again, you can bring their qualities into other relationships as you move forward in your life.

If you work in a team, generate a conversation in your meeting in which everyone recognizes the qualities they see in each other. I don't mean what they do, which is what we usually recognize – the task – I mean the qualities they bring in themselves – their fun, their compassion, their honesty, their courage – whatever it is you see. Listen and feel. Authenticity is something you can feel and hear in the voice. When someone speaks something that is a deep truth to them we know it – it hangs in the air, silencing everything, touching everyone.

Bring emotion into your workplace, in some form or another – emotion is energy, emotion is presence, emotion is real, emotion is life. And it is sorely needed in the modern office.

7

Why? A Reason to Risk

WHY ARE YOU GOING WHERE YOU ARE GOING?

The paycheque? The career? The car? The kudos? Not enough! Not enough to sustain you and keep you healthy and alive.

When you take this level of leadership in your life, and you get access to the reservoirs of energy, and you pick up what you have considered up to now to be responsibility and accountability, it changes into something completely different. It transforms into what can only be described as freedom and joy. I am not saying that it is easy or that it does not demand courage. But energy is released, as you *know* with the surety of the sun coming up tomorrow that what you are doing and where you are going is the right thing for you and the universe. And as your energy is aligned behind your purpose, things fall into your path and other barriers fall away – your congruence reaches others as inspiration and irresistibility – and that moves mountains. This is a level of leadership that is a leadership of attraction – horses and people are drawn to it like a magnet. The horse demands the congruence of our energy and beliefs lined up behind a worthy purpose, but even that isn't enough to sustain. He demands confidence, love, trust and the paradox of dominance through choice not control. The horse asks us to access ourselves in a way that the intellectual world has made us forget.

SWEET DREAMS AND DEMONS

Having had the conference idea, my radar was on for people, experiences, ideas that would be different and demonstrate energy and excitement. I saw an advert in the *Horse and Hound* for a horse show called "Sweet Dreams and Demons" that was to be held in March, a few weeks away. The show was based around Hungarian trick riding, where the riders would hang off the sides of horses, do handstands and jump on and off, whilst their steeds were charging at full gallop. Pretty impressive I thought! I booked a couple of tickets.

The night of the show duly arrived and I took Lizzie, as Steve was not that interested – well neither was Lizzie, but I talked her into a night out.

The "Horsemen of the Apocalypse", as they were called, did their thing, to loud rock music, fire and people dressed like the Ku Klux Klan, and pretty amazing it was too.

I had not really paid attention to the "Sweet Dreams" part of the show as it had not been what had sparked my interest. But that part of the show was now announced.

The tempo of the music changed to a haunting, rhythmical Spanish flamenco, the lights went down and a spotlight carved a circle of light out of the velvet blackness. The audience waited, almost holding its breath. Slowly, a solitary rider on a white, shimmering stallion, the vision of fairytales, walked majestically into the spotlight. The man and horse moved together as one, from one pace to another. I had seen the Spanish riding school, Jeorge, beautiful dressage horses – but I had never seen anything like this! The two acts interchanged throughout the rest of the evening.

The trick riding was impressive, but it paled into the shadow against the dazzling beauty and sheer poetry of the rider and the Spanish stallion. They literally spoke to the audience in some ancient language of music, movement and emotion. Each time they came back, they took the room to another level. A *pas de deux* to the music of *The Mission* will remain with me always – hypnotic and mesmerizing, wanting to hold the moment for ever, liquid gold running though my fingers, its ethereal nature never to be recreated.

Then, finally, the "Garoche" – a tribute to the heritage of the ancient Spanish Doma Vacquera (the hardened Spanish cowboy, who works the plains) – where the rider holds the reins in one hand and in the other he carries a 14 foot long wooden spiked pole. The rider moved the horse under and around the pole in walk and canter, the music changed and built to a crescendo as the two rode impossible canter pirouettes on the spot, moved from full gallop to a standing stop.

The relationship between man and animal, visible and palpable, this was leadership in the moment, as I had never seen it before.

Lizzie and I looked at each other – she knew little of horses, but you didn't need to know anything to know that you were in the presence of genius. We both had tears in our eyes, as had most of the audience. What we had witnessed was not of this world.

There was an interval. We went downstairs to the bathroom. As I was waiting for Lizzie I wandered into the bar area and I noticed a couple of pages of a magazine stuck to the wall. They were tatty and had been there some time. As I read about the trainer who was the subject of the article I began to realize that this man in the article was none other than the amazing genius that I had just been watching seconds ago! Not only that, but he was based in Northamptonshire, at stables that I passed regularly! This was unbelievable.

Of course, I did not approach him that night; I did not have that much courage. But I did try to find his number, without success, for a couple of weeks.

Then one Saturday afternoon, two weeks later, I decided to take the bull by the horns, so to speak, and just go and see him, since I couldn't find his number. I had Holly and Alex with me, but today was the day.

As I arrived at the stables and opened the gate I noticed two men at the top of the long driveway. I opened the gate and drove up the lane. I got to the top and said as I got out of the car, "Are you Peter Maddison-Greenwell?"

"I am" he said.

"I have been looking for you everywhere!"

We talked for an hour or so as Holly and Alex wreaked havoc in his office. They ate oranges and he gave me his handkerchief to wipe their hands – he was OK, was this Peter Maddison-Greenwell.

We came from different worlds in one sense, but from the same place in another. I told him of my plans for the conference and all sorts of stuff, my relationship with riding and my dreams of a horse. We just connected.

He invited me to a show they were doing in London in a couple of weeks.

A few weeks later we were talking on the phone and he asked me whether I was serious about wanting a horse. "Of course" I said aloud, though inside I thought – I've no money and I'm not ready, I can't fit it into my life, but apart from that, yes, I want a horse, a beautiful Spanish stallion!

It's funny when your dreams turn up. It's like you want them on the one hand, but on the other hand you're thinking – Who, me? I'm not ready for this! I am not trained! In fact, I don't know if I'll ever be ready. Our dreams challenge us, deeply.

Peter told me that he had a horse that he was looking to sell, that might be suitable for me – did I want to take a look? Well, I had to, didn't I, to show I was serious.

And I was going to have to go and try this horse – that is to say ride it, in front of people, like I knew what I was doing!

I had spent my life in front of people acting like I knew what I was doing – I was an expert at it. But horses have a knack of showing you up.

When I met Henry for the first time Peter took me into his stable and he was standing against the back wall. He was dark grey, with a thick mane, looking like he had had a bad hair day.

He was not quite the beautiful white horse of my dreams, but I am sure I was not the slim, lithe horsewoman of his dreams either! But there was something about him. He seemed to me like a big old retriever puppy, inquisitive, affectionate, and I liked him immediately as I ran my hands over his dark, warm silky coat.

I made an appointment to come and try him out. His owner was looking for a quick sale and there were a couple of other people coming to see him.

On 7 June at 2.00pm I walked into the arena and quelled my nerves as I mounted the horse. Peter and his colleague Caroline watched from the balcony as I walked and trotted him around. Steering wasn't great but his movement was wonderful, rhythmical, forward going, energetic. I cantered him around in both directions. He was calm, relaxed and I was ecstatic.

I had never done this before in my life, and I had just got on a stallion and gone through all three paces all on my own!

Caroline would comment to me later that she would always remember the first time I ever rode Henry, he was so calm and relaxed. In my world that was all him and not me – but there were others who had ridden him, and he had not been so.

Now I was in real trouble. I had fallen in love with him. He wasn't anything like I had imagined, but I was in love. I had a weekend to talk to Steve… and myself.

I was in absolute turmoil that weekend. It was not the right time, it was too early, next year would be better– apart from the fact I did not have the money I would need to buy him, never mind the mortgage it would cost to keep him – Steve thought I was completely nuts! I mean, he had always known this, but now it was taking the biscuit time! Any sane, logical, rational person would not be having this discussion – that excluded me right away.

By the Monday I had resigned myself to the fact that no matter how much I might love Henry I did not have the money, it was too soon and I would wait a year or so. All very sensible and rational.

I called Peter to tell him so. During the conversation I did mention something about perhaps Henry's owner would consider "loaning" him – that would mean I would take over the monthly upkeep and be able to ride him as if he were mine, I just wouldn't own him outright. Peter said he didn't know, but he would ask.

He called back a couple of hours later to say that this was an option. Oh my god – back on that roller-coaster again.

Now I had to go back home to Steve, and somehow convince him that it was a good idea for me to pay an arm and a leg to keep and train *someone else's* horse. This would be interesting!

To say that the idea did not fly with him is an understatement. I actually presented a written proposal to my own husband of why I should take this opportunity, what I was prepared to give up for it in terms of wine, lotions and potions expenditure and all sorts – I was desperate. I could not pass this opportunity up – to have this beautiful Spanish stallion, with such a wonderful temperament, who was made for me, and to train with this genius of a horseman, who lived on my doorstep – this could not be rejected.

Finally, it was agreed. I would take Henry on a three-month trial, to see how it would work out for us all.

I couldn't afford him, I had no money to buy him, I did not know where the money was going to turn up from to buy him, but there you go. These were a few of the small details that I had left out of my "I want a stallion" dream – you live and learn!

It was three months before my 40th birthday and I had my Spanish stallion, I didn't own him yet, but to all intents and purposes he was mine. A dream had just become reality. I had invented the future, against all the odds. My happiness knew no bounds.

Saturday 6 July 2002

Today has been a perfect day. I feel content, peaceful, as though there need ever be anything else.

This is it – all I ever want...

I rode Henry in the morning and played with the girls in the afternoon and I was as happy as I had ever been in my entire life.

LESSONS I HAVE LEARNED

When I am setting my goals I need to be very, very specific. Because you usually get exactly what you ask for.

When your dreams turn up they often begin to demand more than you believe you are capable of; dreams are wonderful but they are not always easy.

As I move towards my goals I need to let go more and more, just like riding Rocky, by letting go and allowing the energy to flow there is so much more, with so little effort.

Tension and striving disrupts the energy flow in riding just as it does in life.

PRINCIPLES TO LIVE BY

Life will not offer you anything that you cannot deal with in some way or another.

Be specific in what you ask for.

Once your goals are set, let go and trust.

There will be other people who have the other half of your dream – make new friends.

FOR LIFE IN ORGANIZATIONS

The energy and spark of innovation and creativity will not come from the bland, endless rows of hot desk areas, even if you paint the walls purple, put in a cappuccino machine and call it "The Innovation Space". It will come from the loves of your people and how they can bring them to life in their organization. Trust that they are there for a reason, let them fulfil their potential.

In the knowledge age, contribution is not about hours worked it's about contribution made in terms of ideas.

Ideas come from people who are in authentic relationships with people they care about and who care about them.

Ideas can only travel in a network of relationships.

You cannot "performance manage" ideas or emotions. There has to be another way.

EXPANDING YOUR CAPACITY TO LEARN

Do you have some sense of questions emerging in your life?

What are they?

Define one or two of them and then search out in the world to see what you can find.

Search the Internet.

Find some magazines, journals, e-journals, e-libraries.

Go to a big library and see what is on the shelves – what you are drawn to. Talk to people about your question. Follow any leads. Look through this new lens. Investigate your question. See just how many people out there have been looking and questioning, just like you. But notice that their question is never exactly your question. How could it be?

This is something we do not do in organizational life – we expect someone else to come up with the answer to our question and provide us with it from an e-learning system or something – to save time, of course.

This doesn't save time, robbing you of the excitement, of the discovery of your own journey – the particular way you are going to interpret something.

Find out about Action Learning.

And write in your journal about your insights – don't let them slip away.

8

Storm Clouds

And then my world collapsed.

I was sailing with a fair wind, but the storm that had been building over the horizon had been moving and announced its presence overhead with a thunderclap, or more precisely, the trill of my mobile phone.

It was Friday night. I was relaxing with my usual glass of sauvignon blanc. The kids were in bed and it was just one of those moments of settling into the depths of the sofa.

My mobile went off somewhere in the far reaches of my handbag. I retrieved it. It was Perry. This was unusual.

He said he could no longer work on the project; that it was making him ill and that things had come to a head over the last couple of days. Something had happened, to this day I do not know or understand what, but something terrible had happened between him and Mark, and he could not, *would* not, go on. He felt terrible about leaving me and John, but there was nothing I could say that would induce him to continue. He had made this decision, and as awful as it was to let us down, he felt the better for it.

My world fell apart. Perry was an integral part of the whole process. He held a unique space, brought a special presence and energy that no one else could bring. People loved him. John loved him. *I* loved him.

We had more workshops to do – how could we do them without him? How could I go on without him – he was a counter-balance.

Perry said he had written to Mark, and he just wanted to let me know out of courtesy and love that this was what he had to do. Would I wait until Mark contacted me? Of course, Mark and I were speaking almost daily so I did not think it would take long to turn up.

I wrote that night – "It is over before it's begun."

The next thing I had from Mark was a contract that he wanted me to sign, to formalize matters, to protect "us". No word about Perry. I was freaked.

I could not come to terms with the fact that there had been a complete relationship breakdown between two people who were such an integral part of my "family" – it was like my parents had just got divorced and I was supposed to take sides. I mean, the whole thing we were doing was about relationships – so how could this happen? I was emotionally reeling, never mind that I had to deliver six more workshops that I had talked the business into having in the first place and now I was 25% of a facilitator team short!

Mark called about a week later to tell me that he had had a letter from Perry and that he would not be working with us again. According to Mark, Perry was not essential and the arrangement was with his company anyway, not individuals in particular. He asked me about the contract he had sent me. I said that we would not be signing his contract, but that John was working with our procurement people to produce a business contract that would include our terms as well as his.

Monday 8 July 2002

> I am not comfortable – it doesn't matter what happened between them – the fact is something did, and everything is up for question. Trouble is… he's lost me in the long term – my core value is connection and it has been violated – and it is not something that can be restored because trust with me is absolute – all or nothing.

The next workshop approached and I headed off to Stow with heaviness in my soul, a weight that I could not fully articulate. I just had to keep going somehow, I was leading this for my business and I just had to hold it together. As I arrived at the arena tears welled up in the back of my throat; this was going to be tough.

There was a subtle shift in the dynamics of the facilitator group. The depth and trust in relationships was no longer there – how could it be? And I am sure that this had an effect on the group. Added to this, there was no longer a counter-balance to Mark.

Despite the tensions of the session, we all got through it. The scores were not as high as they had been on previous workshops, there was not the same sense of breakthrough, but some of the delegates did generate new insights for themselves.

Instinctive alarm bells were firing everywhere in my system. Where I thought I was going and what I thought I was doing seemed to be sinking in quicksand. The relationships between the facilitators were fundamental but now there was something at the heart of things that could not be spoken. As a result the energies could not fully flow in the workshop, and tensions were reflecting everywhere.

Tuesday 21 May 2002

I realize that I have not been allowing myself to experience my own pain, to acknowledge the things that have hurt me most in my life – because my capacity to feel is so intense the depths are not to be plummeted.

I have pushed away my pain, made it invalid, if it is not so for others – denying myself, my needs – too selfish, self-indulgent – echoes of my childhood. Intense and passionate – it's the dark and the light – my mother's death – I am still not reconciled, because there was no one for me to grieve with – I was holding it together for everyone else, there was no one to hold me.

The loneliness of my mother, now I know her and she is not here and I'll never know her. The greatest pains in my life are in the midst of my relationships, my connections – or when the connections are broken.

It's funny, the words come back to me from the workshop – "love", "caring", "nurturing" – from the core of who I am – and that is who I am – and that is my motivation – and I have never really accepted that as true. I always thought that I never gave enough in my relationships – and it's not about that – it's a being – it's a force, it is power and it is pain too – that's why I experience emotion with it – because by its essence it carries pain.

Wednesday 29 May 2002

I lean over the edge of a virtual precipice. A new portal that has been invisible to me previously has just opened up before me and I lean in and look. I recognize that for most of my life I have been holding myself together. I use the term pain because that's what it feels like. Many times I felt it and pushed it away, denied myself its embrace, denied myself the validity, understanding and forgiveness of that pain, and blocked myself in the process. Blocked the very essence of me, the capacity to experience pain, the deep way that I could. It's almost like I don't know how in one way, and in another the fear of the dam bursting and not being able to stop it, not knowing where it might take me, and if I will be OK there. Also, there's a part of me that denies the reality of the pain – judges my tears – and then in the judging of the tears denies the hurt that brings them – resists it so it comes again and again. I am not through it.

When things don't go my way I distance myself – run away mentally, emotionally, physically. I feel that beginning the Alexander Technique will bring me back to my own. The work with my coach Ann will reconnect me with my dark side and help me to accept all parts of me, taking me through some of the areas I have denied.

I feel stiller since I began the Alexander Technique – I can't quite explain...

We did two more workshops but the original ease and depth of trust amongst the group had disappeared. As often happens at this point in the year, budgets come under scrutiny, as the business seeks to manage its year-end position. My boss had asked me to take a good look at the learning and development spend, with a view to trimming it. This was not an unusual occurrence and I always approach it from the point of view of how we can achieve the same or better results with less resources. There was a fairly heavy squeeze so we had to consider everything – even the leadership programme – perhaps postpone some of the work until next year or collapse a few workshops.

One more workshop was completed. Further rifts emerged within the team that led to some difficult times for all of us, and that seemed to be that. A sudden end to this wonderful work, like a beautiful firework that lights up the sky for an instant and then fades into the darkness once more.

Wednesday 11 September 2002

I feel very sad tonight. I had to go into my email and delete loads of messages – so much of it meaningless drivel, meaningless to me anyway. I need some meaning and I find it in real conversations.

Watching the documentaries about the Twin Towers tragedy last year I am so struck by all those innocent people who died at work – they died at their computers and desks – I hope it had some meaning for them – good meaning. People have heart attacks, they panic, are stressed – what we do in my department – we are the people who try to help. To help them when they are deeply stuck, when there is nowhere to turn. It's like we try to throw them a life-line, if they can hear us. We are healers in a way.

Yes, we link it to performance, but that is not what I really mean, that is an excuse. It's a cross between something spiritual and something medical, because the body, the mind and the soul are all in the one place at the same time… maybe there is a need for a new concept in Human Resources – something deeper… as I deleted those emails I felt like resigning. As I contemplate some things ahead, I think I cannot live into this meaningless, constructed, façade. There must be meaning for me.

LESSONS I HAVE LEARNED

Sometimes in my desire to keep going, to keep pursuing my dreams, I ignore any little crack or question that might stop me. This is going to turn up anyway, so I may as well deal with it.

In times of severe stress the old patterns turn up again; I need to find holding strategies that will allow me movement.

This leadership thing is not a "one time sorted it" kind of deal – you keep having to work at it, falling down and getting up again one more time.

Relationships must hold truth of a kind, a deeper bond, to be able to hold the course when the going gets tough.

Pain is a part of my life, as much as joy, it is a part of me – the one cannot exist without the other. It has to be given its place, it has to be experienced and expressed.

PRINCIPLES TO LIVE BY

What is achieved comes out of the authenticity of the relationship.

Dreams, positive intentions, positive thinking do not mean the denial of problems, pain, fear or uncertainty. These feelings must be recognized, acknowledged and expressed. They are a part of you.

The problems and pain are all a part of movement, guiding you and taking you somewhere else.

FOR LIFE IN ORGANIZATIONS

If people in your organization can express their pain as well as their joy, there will be strength and depth in the relationship, and in the business.

People need time and space to get through. At this time they need your constant unconditional support, not exclusion or being left alone. The problems of a relationship cannot be solved outside of that relationship.

EXPANDING YOUR CAPACITY TO LEARN...

At a time that feels appropriate begin to write about the times, moments and events that have caused you pain, that have been tough for you. And as you have been doing just allow your writing to flow, even though you may not know what you are going to write before your pen touches the page. We are so conditioned by our education to seek an already stored answer somewhere in the computer we consider to be our memory or brain, and for that answer to come out, coherent, factual, fully formed and unarguable. Then we spend our time seeking evidence to support it and defend it – to make us right. And all this keeps us where we are; yes, it sustains our personality in one respect, but holds us back in another. Just expressing what you feel to yourself, allowing yourself to hear, feel and see it, in a safe environment, will allow you to generate movement for yourself.

And that will be what it will be and it will take the time that it will take. You do not have to be held by the patterns of your past, if you want something different, but neither can they be denied.

Inner and Outer Alignment – Do You Really Mean It?

Is everything lining up for you? Is your voice speaking what your heart is feeling, no matter what? And is your body taking that step? Is it real – outside and inside?

You cannot get to this stage of engagement with the horse and not begin to get a sense of how you have been restraining yourself. You suddenly become startlingly aware of the silent voices in your head that have told you all your life – "You can't do that", "You're not worth that" or "What will everyone else think?" You hear the voices and you realize that you are saying these things to yourself and then, guess what? You get to say, to use Richard Bandler's famous expression, "Shut the f*** up!" Try it – they really don't like it.

Just as those thoughts hold you back so they hold the horse back. Why would the horse want to connect with that energy? And you get to say something different, like – "I can do this", "I am worth this", "I can have this".

When you move into the present living moment you really don't care what anyone else thinks because you are being truthful to yourself. The relationship with the animal shows how we allow ourselves and others to constrain our possibilities and then we act into these constraints as though they were true. In reaching into ourselves to find the congruence of who we really are we glimpse the possibilities that lie there. And we can choose. When you add to this the discovery that there is truly only the living moment, and even that is based upon how we interpret it, everything is up for grabs.

Life moved on from the drama of those summer months and I moved forward to concentrate on my work in the business. Through my work with the horses, and the subsequent reading that I had been doing, I wanted to create a new paradigm of leadership and learning in the business – something that would be more real than many of the corporate platitudes of those huge change programmes – something that gave people permission to be who they are, to figure out what they had to bring and how they could work together in real relationships, not structure charts. The role of learning, leadership and development had been expanding and expanding throughout the whole organization. It had moved from the dusky backwaters of Human Resources into a fairly cool and funky place to be – we did fun stuff and it worked! We had implemented our strategy, our principles and beliefs and everywhere people were feeling the benefits – it was fabulous.

One day I was sitting in a meeting with my boss Peter and a new colleague who had just joined the department. I was trying to articulate what we were trying to do with learning, leadership and development, that for me it was all about accessing and releasing the energy of every individual in the business. I was in full flow on my principles and I was describing my experience of moving Maddie that day in the ménage. I stopped mid-flow, as you often do when you are seeking the exact word to express something that is beyond the ability of language to capture. I was describing the moment when I became completely congruent and aligned and I felt the energy flow out from me – and what I experienced as a consequence of it – I said, "I felt completely… Unstoppable!"

Now there's a word!

That one word captured it all. Because once you have that alignment built upon your own commitments, nothing and no one can stop you, it's just stuff.

Our people strategy had just been born. And as with many other ideas that arrive like this, I was to discover later that not only did the idea of "Unstoppable People" already exist but I was to meet and work with the author of the book of the same name, Adrian Gilpin, an individual who shared many of my philosophies and beliefs.

"Individual and Organizational Transformation through Unstoppable People – A New Paradigm in Learning and Leadership" – I put it everywhere, and before long it was turning up all by itself!

Cool! Then it became one of the five key strategies of the business and had been invented by the board – that's when you know you are making progress.

This was fantastic, because with a people strategy entitled "Unstoppable People" you can do just about anything!

And it set the stage and established the frame for energy and a different approach to learning, leadership and development that, by the way, we had already begun.

As I mentioned earlier, I was doing interviews with a number of the individuals who had participated in the equine leadership programmes. I had found a type of interview called "phenomenonological" – don't worry, Microsoft Word doesn't recognize it either! What the individuals had experienced with the horses was a unique phenomenon, a unique experience for them, and I wanted to explore it in as open a way as possible. To understand what they made of it, what they got from it and if they had generated any changes in their lives as a result.

The interview is unstructured and can go in whatever direction emerges – it allows the interviewee and the interviewer to both participate in the conversation, questioning, exploring, inquiring, understanding, learning – whatever. The interviews were taped so that the interviewer could really listen and participate, without having to think about taking notes. There were a number of us from my team doing the interviews, to allow a greater breadth of inquiry.

I could not help but learn with each interview – it was fascinating.

Using these observations I had begun to formulate my own approach to using horses as a method to generate sustainable learning and change.

The first thing I noticed was that, in many cases, there had been fundamental changes that had made a great impact on people's lives – the way they looked at everything! It wasn't about one aspect or one particular skill – it was deeper than that. For many it had been a life-changing experience, as it had been for me.

There was another workshop we were running at that time called "You Can If You Think You Can", run by a very powerful and motivational speaker. This workshop was very uplifting. Its design was around motivational speaking, inspirational stories and things to think about in your own life – particularly around work-life balance.

It did not require delegates to learn experientially, it did not take them out of their comfort zone. Everyone, to a man, loved this workshop and it was much talked about in the business – it was a powerful signal as to what was important about working here. It was great – nothing to argue with there.

The horse work was much deeper, yet hardly anyone talked about it in groups of more than two, or when they did it was some sort of hearty guffaw about the chanting thing! It was too deep, too personal, too revealing to say you had had a major insight that had changed your life, because that would have implied that there had been something wrong with your life in the first place.

And if you admitted you got something out of it – well maybe you were OK with that chanting stuff – and that would put you in a very funny place!

Because of the lack of open debate, it would have been easy to believe that the horse work had not been as successful. I was interested to discover that Carl Rogers, the father of person-centred therapy, had also noted how when groups first get together they will most often talk about negative themes first, by way of testing whether it is safe to speak, before revealing more positive aspects, which tend to leave one more vulnerable in revealing oneself.

It was also becoming clear to me that, despite working with teams and taking them to new depths in their relationships, this understanding was not sustained back in the work environment, despite the fact that it was recognized to be beneficial. The prevailing context proved to be too strong, and it was becoming clear that the group dynamics could kill the possibility of learning before it had a chance to take root. The teams needed more ongoing support than I had anticipated. I had naively thought that if you changed the individual, you changed the organization. I did not foresee that changing the prevailing patterns of relationships in the organization was going to take more than a two-day programme, even if it had been transformational.

It was almost as though people expected something to change them from the outside, without them doing anything, and if it didn't work like that then the process didn't work! I was beginning to realize that deep insight requires ongoing support. People could avoid learning by failing to create the necessary space or attention to do it; they could keep things comfortable. A single moment could change someone's life, but they had to engage with it in that way. Two days was not going to transform anything if the individuals in the team were not engaged and committed to some kind of change.

Again and again I saw the opportunity for learning and innovation being sub-optimized. Individuals were not taking full responsibility for their capacity to learn, and then to change, to embody and be different. They were often passive, waiting for someone or something to do it for them. Just like we are taught at school – the person at the front of the room is supposed to tell you stuff in an easy to understand format. And if you don't understand it *they* need to change it so you do!

In some cases there was so much fear of emotion – which was the very access point to their own and others' energy. In other cases individuals saw the power of emotion and connection and were using it in their teams to generate extraordinary results.

It was out of this thinking that I began to understand what leadership and "Unstoppable People" was all about – well I knew what it was all about, I just hadn't been able to articulate it yet. One of the key aspects was all about accelerating the capacity to learn, enabling individuals to understand that they alone were responsible for their learning, not the facilitator, the author, the speaker, anybody else – only them. The other thing I began to recognize about learning was that is was a deeply personal, holistic process that involved challenging some of our long-held constructs of how we see the world. It was not about the digesting of information and the ability to regurgitate it. I had written in my diary "My responsibility for my own learning, interpretation is everything. I am not 'developed' by something outside me – I have to re-visit it, call it up, think about it – re-interpret – use my insight as a resource – be my insight…"

Everyone liked this Unstoppable People thing, but they wanted to know what it looked like – what were the skills, the competencies? Who was an unstoppable person and who wasn't? Er??

Then, it began to have babies – "unstoppability" and "creating an unstoppable environment" – interesting, I thought, but missing the point. The word came from the experience of a human energy force, the connection of mind, body and energy.

An environment cannot be "unstoppable", it's an abstract concept! And it doesn't have energy. Get to the people who construct and live the environment moment by moment.

"Unstoppability" is not a characteristic that can be separated from the person and their desires, it emerges as a consequence of the engagement of the person with their desires – it cannot be measured independently.

But I had begun to understand what it was I was seeking to articulate and communicate. I went back to moments with the horses. Time and time again, as I was coaching, I would see the individual move to the edge, the point of frustration where nothing they were trying was working, then something would occur to them – I could do this? Their faces would light up with a new idea, so in a microsecond the learning had occurred, but that is not enough.

It has to be acted upon in order to truly learn and know, from the other side of the experience – a faltering, unsure, embodied step – energy and movement – they had to *do* something, risk themselves. They had to act into the universe, without knowing the future consequences of their actions. The horse would let them know if it had worked or not, if they meant it, if it was fully embodied or not. That gap between insight and action was often the smallest step, a new thought, a different touch, but it was also a precipice they could not see beyond, a cavern of unknown depths, with no hand to hold, no rope to guide, only the invisible thread of trust in themselves. And here was the point of leadership, of hesitant belief in self, alone to overcome and move forward.

Leadership and "Unstoppable People" was about:

The capacity to learn

The energy to act, and

The courage to lead – all in the same energetic instant.

At the conclusion of the horse programmes I had a period of licking my own wounds, a period of just letting things die down. Thinking about it all continued to bring some pain for me and triggered a number of uncomfortable questions. I had a lot going on so I did not think about it too much. I was taking the overall leadership strategy forward in a number of other exciting ways. All the while though I carried a question – How was I going to continue to do this work with horses when I had lost the relationship with the individual who had been my partner in all of this; how could I continue on my own? I could see no way to move forward, just some kind of suspension.

I had been invited to speak at a number of conferences that year. You will remember from my goals that I had said that I had wanted to be a speaker and commentator on leadership and so that is what had turned up. Through a number of different conversations I was invited to speak at three conferences – one on e-learning, one on the subject of talent and one on the subject of leadership. I didn't seek them out, they just came along.

Now secretly I also had this crazy idea of taking some horses along to a conference about leadership and had determined that I would do this somewhere in the far off future, that I would obviously need to hire Wembley Stadium. This was one of those ideas that was a little bit edgy so I had not actually got to the point of daring to utter it to anyone else beyond my immediate team. But the guy who had invited me to speak was a fun, open, easy sort of person and had very quickly recognized that I was a bit strange, in that I did things very differently to many HR/Learning people he had met, so we would have a laugh. In the midst of one of these conversations I jokingly said that one day I was going to take horses to a conference about leadership to demonstrate real leadership in moment by moment action. He said, thoughtfully, "Well, actually, Imperial College in London has a bit of grass area, in a sort of courtyard... maybe you could do it there?"

I nearly fell off my seat in excitement. This wasn't years away, this was in a couple of months!

And so the wheels were set in motion to see if this would be a possibility.

The conference organizers liked the idea. The guy who owned the grass was not so sure. After all, it was the kind of grass that had a "Keep Off The Grass" sign on it – so you can understand why he wasn't too happy about bringing a couple of horses down to churn it all up (in his imagination). I had to sign my life away – it was on, it was off, it was on – the weather? What if it rained? But, the day dawned – one of those rare Indian summer days in mid-September – it was perfect.

I had worked on my conference presentation for weeks, the structure was good, the content refreshing. I had worked on my own state and rehearsed until I was word perfect. I could even recite a poem from memory. I donned a white suit and felt fantastic. I did my thing for 45 minutes in the conference hall and then all 400 people walked out to the sunshine and stood around the grass watching the riders and horses (and Flamenco dancers) move and dance to the rhythm of the Spanish guitars.

As I stood watching the demonstration, looking into the faces of the delegates, I thought – I am here, I made all this happen, this was my dream and here I am.

Tuesday 17 September 2002

Today is one of those days I never want to end, like my wedding day. I can't really take it all in. The conference today was spectacular – well for me anyway. So many friends came to be with me. Caroline, Kellyn, Lesley, Connie, Jane B and Jane N, Perry, Terry (at the last minute) and so many people came up to me, with emotion in their faces – inspiring, thank you again and again, even those not so confident, who did not usually do such things – I connected with them. I could have stood on that platform and talked Swedish; it wouldn't have made much difference. I just shone – I reached out to them with an energy, with an openness and confidence and... a permission, that they were fine.

And then to the horses – to see all those people standing around waiting and watching – and the people in the buildings, on the street, everywhere – mesmerized by what they saw.

It's funny that at the time of daring to dream the dream seems so distant, but in the moment of attainment it is just one small step, just the next step, the next breath.

Today is one of those special days when I can't believe my life and the riches and treasures heaped upon me. Today had meaning.

Despite what I felt to be the complete collapse of my leadership work with horses, the pain and doubts that it brought, I continued to move forward. In one sense I had to distance myself, in order that I would find my own courage, my own faith in myself, and not continue to be reliant upon others.

I had to lead, no matter what. I had to face the test. I had to mean it with everything, in such a way that nothing would hold me back, nothing would stop me – one way or another I would continue to move forward in my unfolding journey to discover where it was taking me.

Monday 11 November 2002

I will go forward with the work that I have to do, that is my journey, my destiny, my life… I am getting very busy again and I need to prioritize and try and live in my week, my day, my hour, my minute.

Just to be – not to suffer the fluctuations of ego – it's not for me, or about me, I am a messenger, I am a voice, I have to say things that are my responsibility, but that is not who I am. I am who listens to me speak. I am the child, the essence, the source, the arms in the middle of the night, the stillness, the peace, the enoughness that I am sensing from time to time at the moment.

I am enough, this is enough – oh I know I have my plans – and I know they will come – but they are not what sustain me, they are not me.

The relationships I have are me and how I extend myself to others and what I offer them to step into as a possibility.

Filling my day with positive, nurturing, loving, enquiring relationships – moving away from those that drain me.

LESSONS I HAVE LEARNED

Learning is about when things go wrong, not when they go right. When things go according to plan or, more accurately, *seem* to go according to plan, the constructs of your mind remain intact. There is no serious challenge to them, and therefore no change. Learning comes from engaging in the challenge to your internal world; this is a gift that we so often refuse to open.

My role in life is not to "fix" anybody, only to support those who are seeking something else. I am not responsible for their learning, only my own.

Deep learning needs ongoing support. The new conversation needs to be nurtured, not shut away in a dark, silent cupboard.

Deep learning requires processing and integrating into the constructs of self. This takes time and it takes space and it takes courage.

Deep learning also requires the unshakeable, unconditional acceptance of a number of people who love you and believe in you, no matter what.

What we say, what we hear others say to us, what they really mean – none of this is as coherent as you might think.

I have to find my own way forward, not live into a pale imitation of someone else.

Somehow, when I speak and talk about my dreams, they turn up a lot faster than I anticipate – this can range from being disconcerting to down right scary.

PRINCIPLES TO LIVE BY

Act, speak, move, do something.
Be with people who love you, you will sustain each other.
After the pain move on, seek growth.
Hold on, no matter what, hold on.

FOR LIFE IN ORGANIZATIONS

If your organization is seeking true innovation then do not expect it to be perfect first time, second time or even third time. Do not just look and focus on what went wrong, focus on what was learned and celebrate that. Take it and use it.

Creating completely new thoughts, businesses, markets means that we need to go to the very edge of our thinking, we need to be able to hang out in that space of discomfort where none of what you know makes sense.

EXPANDING YOUR CAPACITY TO LEARN...

Have you begun to notice that writing in your journal is shaping your life differently? Really, the writing that you are doing is about training yourself to think in a different way, a way that can create a different level of awareness in your life, a way that lets you look at your own thoughts and think – Is that a sensible way to look at this issue? Is this helping me?

Look at your journal, re-read it – what do you notice?

Will I Go With You?

Do I want to go with you because you are important, because you have a nice suit, because I am afraid of you? Or maybe it's because I think you are better than me, or worse than me? Why? Why do you sometimes need to be with someone, it's a physical thing, a need, just to be in his or her presence? What is that and how much of it do we have in organizations?

You don't build a relationship with a horse over the telephone, via email or any of the other tools of "remote working". I wonder what makes us think that human beings can do this?

Research suggests that 7% of communication is in the words – what of the other 93%? The exchange with the horse begins to help us understand this.

We engage people with our eyes, our hands and our voice as its energy waves wrap around the person we are with. They can feel our energy field, are affected by it and reach out to us in return. Our very thoughts create movement in the energy field. What level of power are you using? What level of love? What level of openness? Closure? The relationship with the horse offers us a window into the dynamic world of relationships and how we are constructing ourselves against the other's response in our every gesture. You can see that mobility can be yours.

Why?

This is often a question that is missing in many company vision statements. A real "why". A "why" that could offer some meaning for our lives. That we could connect to, a reason to give of ourselves, that is beyond shareholder value, beyond a profit percentage growth target. It seems that businesses have lots of "whats" – to become Number One in this, to make the most of that, to be the biggest of the other. You can have a "what" but unless there is a personal "why" you will hear that expression "We've got to get their hearts and minds" – oh yes, and how are you going to do that? A fancy presentation? A pretty card? Cascade workshops?

My colleague John coined a beautiful expression; "Vision is an experience that you belong to…"

There has to be that sense of belonging, otherwise how can you contribute? But belonging is a two-way street – it is a shaping together, a coming together, a bending and changing – not a sign-up to the plan or a "get on another train, this one's leaving the station!" You know the sort of thing.

These are the statements that are often used by executives who are posturing and pretending they are tough leaders – that's not tough – tough is having the conversation with the people who don't believe in you, understanding why, changing your plan, so that they can belong – anything else is just pretend.

And do these leaders for one minute imagine that the people who have got on the train are the ones they need? Oh no, they are just the ones who will play the game, as it suits them, until such time as that leader's plan does not fit their agenda any more. Leadership here is a very lonely place – if you are the only one with a "why".

As I began to work with energy, I began to run my team meetings differently. In fact, I began to engage in meetings *per se* in a totally different way. But let's begin with my team meetings. First of all I invited everyone who was in the group, no matter what level they were – manager, secretary or administrator, it was not important. Just a little thing, but people began to belong, belong in a sense that was greater than their job title and where they sat in the hierarchy.

And we did agendas, well, one of the members would create an agenda and circulate it, but I would always write one up on the flipchart at the beginning of the meeting in live, sprawling colour – and whatever we needed to talk about would always turn up. It was a way of connecting, checking in – clean, tidy words on a piece of paper did not do it.

Then the first thing that we would do in the meeting was to go around the table and hear from every person about something fantastic or amazing that had happened in any part of their lives in the past week or month, or since we had last met. This sort of request is invariably met with silence, until someone can bear the discomfort no longer and begins to replace it with another type of discomfort, tentatively, apologizing for the small nature of their joy, that it wouldn't mean anything to anyone else but it meant something to them... an exam in nutrition taken and passed, a 13-year old daughter who had published a heartfelt poem, a workshop that had reached into someone's soul, an acknowledgement from another function in the business, a painting completed, a small step on the fulfilment of a dream... As each individual spoke, their words were connected to something of great importance to them and would access their joy and their achievement as they saw their impact reflected back in the faces of the others around the table. They would sit a little more upright in their chairs; there was a hint of greater confidence. They would begin to belong at a deeper level of who they were and what they believed in and what was important to them.

They were speaking about their world and there was a group of people listening. And then our eyes would moisten as we would hear one of our group describe achieving some stretching task that they did not quite believe they could achieve, though we all knew they would fly. We would hear and support them becoming more of who they were, and see the magic and possibility that belonging and acceptance could bring.

This was about energy, accessing it, generating it, sustaining it – it wasn't about the things we did necessarily, it was about the way it made us feel in that group, in that meeting, in that moment. And we would carry this through the meeting; or rather it would carry us – a wave of unstoppability. Here we created a very deep "why". It was a "why" that meant to us – we help people grow, no matter what.

That's the vision, it's that simple and we don't need to write it down, and I belong to it in a way that any action I take will be aligned to this principle.

It was a *why* that meant I belonged to this special group that lets me make my unique contribution. It was a *why* that was because *I believe in you as you believe in me...* and when you get to this level of *why* not only do people want to go with you they want to take you where it is you want to go...

That year I had gone on holiday with the family to Greece. It was all inclusive – and the best, best thing of all – there were kids clubs so for the first time in almost five years I was going to be able to sit by a pool and read a book or not, as the notion took me! Now, this will sound really odd to people who do not have children, but take it from me, this was sheer luxury, even if it was only for a couple of hours a day! Believe me, 22 hours a day is enough children for anybody – you may think I exaggerate but no, when there's two of them they can alternate the night waking so you get as little sleep as possible which, after a while, changes your personality!

One afternoon, as I sat by the pool, I decided to write down my goals in detail. Everything I wanted in my life over the next 10 years, when I would achieve it, what it would be like, leaving no stone unturned. It was as I was doing this that the idea of a "Life Navigation" system first occurred to me – a second generation time management system, only it wasn't going to be about time or "to do" lists, it was going to be about creating the identity you wanted to become and leading the life you wanted to lead – it was about life, love and leadership. It was about finding the source of your own energy, the source of your own unique contribution – not just what other people wanted you to get done for them. Because stress comes when we are out of alignment, when our activities are not aligned to what really matters to us. And I had seen for myself the stress held in the bodies of the individuals that I had worked with in the workshop – I had seen their bodies frozen with tension, weary with exhaustion. And I had seen their physiology change as they worked to understand what they really wanted in their lives. The solution to work-life balance was not a question of balance at all, it was a question of finding what it is you love to do, that when you do it gives you energy and doesn't take it away. I wanted to integrate an individual's purpose with their learning, and their energy – because in this way the universe would come to meet them, and they would feel alive.

So many people I had met along the way had touched and inspired me. I remember working with a sales guy on one particular workshop. There was an odd number in the group so I was working through one of the exercises with him. It was about what he wanted in his future. He had his eyes closed and he was taking his first step along his future time-line – he said, "I want to not be afraid when the phone rings… I want to not start the week on a low because it is Monday and end it on a high because it is Friday…"

What he said struck me to my core. Tears were in my voice – here was a successful person on the surface – as we all pretend to be – but on another level here was a person dying a little at a time. And I knew all too well the ring tone he was talking about, I knew that place of wading through molasses, day in day out, just thinking about getting to Friday, but with not enough self-esteem and energy to change the whole thing.

Each time I doubted that I was heading in the right direction I would think of this man, and many others like him, who would sit across tables in small meeting rooms with their eyes moist – finally finding someone to talk to who did not judge them for their fears, someone who would just listen, and in the speaking and listening, magic would happen – their situation would transform. These were the secret demons that we hide from our leaders and superiors, lest they judge us and find us wanting, as we find ourselves wanting. It amazes me the amnesia of many leaders who, once in place, deny the existence of such a dark place.

Again, I did not know how I would do this; I only knew that I would. This would be how I would share my learning and experience with anyone else that it might help. I cemented several of my other intentions, but this was the major breakthrough that I made – how I was going to take my work forward into the world. I had something to say, and I was going to say it!

I love books. I love bookstores, libraries, other people's bookcases, Amazon – anything to do with books I just adore. As a child I read every Enid Blyton book ever written, followed by every Agatha Christie, several times. It was not until I began engaging in Action Learning, however, that books took on a different meaning for me. In school and education you are told what books to read – like they know what your real questions are! Well, they do, because they have supplied you with the questions and the answers. There's just the small matter of engagement and the fact that the future is different from the past, so any question is by definition a new question, so how could it be answered by information from the past?

The written word dies on the page until it is engaged with anew by a new adventurer, who in their reading transforms the ancient word into a new thought, an energetic thought in their own minds – and it comes to life again, but never in quite the same way. Knowledge is dynamic, perpetually moving, transforming with each person who engages in the quest to understand their world.

This was the basis that I engaged with books – they were not books. They were people and ideas, and the book was my way of being able to discover the thinking, the discoveries of another person's life.

Where books were concerned, I followed my nose. I'd find one book that would say something completely new and fresh to me, that made sense to me in my everyday experience – I saw or felt or heard it to be true – it enlightened me, it helped me, it changed me, because that was the way I engaged with it – these weren't dead words page after page, this was treasure that could transform my life, the secrets of the universe.

I devoured books. Despite having a job, two children, a horse and running a home, when I got hold of one of these books I would swallow it whole – reading it in a weekend, in early mornings and late evenings, whenever I could grasp a minute. I underlined anything that spoke to me, scrawling all over it – this was knowledge creation in action not some artefact to be preserved like a museum piece. The only thing a book was worth was what I was going to do with it.

The reason I began a doctorate straight after I had finished a Masters degree was because I missed the learning, I missed having a reason to read and integrate new knowledge into my experience and experiment and find out new stuff and new people all the time – I would find whole concepts and theories and ideas I never even had an inkling existed. Once you become attuned to this many ideas everything is possibility – the answer or a new question would just be around the next corner, or rather in the next delivery from Amazon. And after the reading the thinking – in the bath, on the motorway, all the time, processing and connecting one idea to another idea. Because the thing is you see, in the problems that I needed to solve all the possible ideas had not been put in the same place yet – because no one had ever had the same question that I had had – just like no one has ever had the exact same question that you have.

My central question was about leadership, what was it really? And the question did not come from some abstract academic idea that I had to read up on, it came from the moment when I had moved Maddie with the power of my own mind. I had to understand how I had been able to move this creature from 15 feet away, and if this was possible what else was possible? It came from the reality of my own life and my own struggles to integrate my life, to find my own way in the world.

Monday 15 July 2002

The essay on loneliness struck me, hard. A chord resonated somewhere in my mind. Why am I doing this doctorate? Validation? Security? It is a deeper inquiry than equine-based coaching or leadership – much deeper than this. It is this validation, or not being valid, my experience, my desires, my hopes and dreams as not being valid in a male ordered world. I am still carrying this weight – I thought I had put it to bed – but it will not lie down and die – there is something deep within me screaming about the silence that women must suffer. Maternity policies that treat you as if you have no value, while you create life itself. The loneliness of being a woman in meeting after meeting populated by men – and the need to do something outstanding to be heard, to be there, to be valid.

My voice, I keep talking about my voice.

The words are not the experience, they never can be – they are but an echo, a shadow.

Monday 5 August 2002

Maybe it's this – maybe it's the reality of leadership that I want to challenge – the inner dialogue, the doubts, the struggle – the stuff that is denied and nowhere to be found in the models or frameworks, because we dare not speak about it.

I read books on energy, on quantum mechanics, healing, emotions, learning, therapy, classical riding, horse-whispering, the Alexander

Technique, Hellerwork, Rolfing, Radionics, Remote Viewing, Kinesiology, NLP, thought field therapy, learning, chaos, physics, spirituality, transformation, consciousness, evolutionary psychology, leadership, human social dynamics, meaning, time, relationships, conversation – anything that might cast some light on what happened that day in the ménage.

And poetry – sometimes no science can capture the essence of human experience, only the poet can reach into the depths of the human soul and articulate truth that needs no proof. I discovered David Whyte, a rare gift to the literary world. His books are the ones I return to again and again, the elegance and truth of the ideas he expresses, his words like a fine wine, of which I never tire.

What follows is in essence the meaning and sense I made of what I read, and how it shaped my interpretation not only of what I saw and felt working with horses but also of what I saw and felt in all aspects of my life.

There were a number of key themes that ran throughout all the books and articles that I read...

CORE SPIRIT

There was something about the core spirit, the essence or energy of a human being. Here leadership was an inner, personal journey of the discovery of one's own unique talents and place in the world. This is the source of inspiration. Aspects of our behaviour cannot be split out from the whole. The shadow side must be embraced as part of the journey. Expressing the self takes great courage.

EMOTIONS

Emotions were key to everything, underlie everything, even as we deny them in rational and logical language. There is no such thing as objective thought. Emotional responses occur before intellectual thought. The body is the unconscious mind and the neuropeptide is the transformational thought. Repressed emotions are stored in the body. Body-mind therapies focus on freeing up the emotions. There is an emotional connection to health and/or illness. Emotions are often denied/suppressed in modern organizational life.

BELIEFS

The will to live is not an abstraction. Hope is a biochemical exchange.

HUMANITY

We are of nature, it is our essential way of being – and yet we deny it. There is a need in business for the timeless qualities of wisdom, spirit, heart.

AWARENESS

We are always radiating our awareness out into the world – whatever we send out, we get back.

We do not always learn from what happens to us. Awareness is everything in learning.

We must become aware of the shadow and what it has to teach us.

CONSCIOUSNESS

There are many layers of consciousness. Consciousness may be held within the energy field itself, not just in our awareness of it. Intention may be accessing layers of consciousness. Ordinary perception is very limited in its capability. Precognition information is available. Intention can act upon seed moments, even if they were in the past.

MEDITATION

Meditation slows down the functions of the body, in particular the mind, and is the gateway to higher levels of consciousness. It gets beyond the "grosser" levels of the body, where consciousness can have an effect. Force does not achieve its ends – letting go and gentle wishing. Here is access to the living moment.

CONTRADICTIONS OF THE MODERN WORLD

The impact of our environment challenges our health. Solutions to save money put considerable strain upon the human organism, as they strip away relationship.

The staged, perfectly imagined, processed, socially polite, political, power-based world of organizational life is a source of stress. Organizations seek to create change on the rational and cognitive level where there is little energy and emotion is not required. This is not the level for change. If there is no energy there can be no movement.

Complexity guru Ralph Stacey takes us to the living moment. He suggests that relationships socially construct individual minds and selves. Meaning is dynamically created and identity constructed. Past relationship patterns constrain but the opportunity to change is always present. The body as a whole is central as the social process includes feelings and emotions and gesture is in the whole body (and energy field).

Stacey challenges the linear model of organizational life. He notes that even when double loop learning has taken place, the context re-constructing itself may be too strong for the individual to resist. Play can hold creative anxiety. Leaders can be the creation of the group that they lead. There is no static outside.

Stressed and depressed people lower their immune response – they weaken their DNA's ability to heal itself.

How human beings really are…

We are influenced by past patterning, our past experience and how we interpret it. The patterns act as lenses through which we interpret our current experience. Meaning is dynamically created, as we make sense of incoming information and our identities are re-constructed to maintain familiarity. The private self and the public self are not the same. We begin from our experience – not anyone else's.

Aural speech is a sensuous flow of patterned feeling – the somatic (body feeling) and the primordial are present.

People are influenced at the somatic level. Human beings are very influenced by context – our behaviour and our personality are not as stable as we would like to believe. The social dynamics of the organization may hold restraining dynamics that work against personal growth.

ENERGY

Illness appears in the energy field first.

Every thought is a small outcropping in the electromagnetic field.

Our bodies know what is good for us.

Fields of congruent energy have greater influence.

In the energy field small changes make a big difference.

The body can respond to conditions before the mind.

All living things produce an energy field.

The biophysical body is a quantum field and can therefore be in two places simultaneously.

Rolfing and Hellerwork create energy flow and alignment in the body-mind.

Healers seem to give off surges of energy. Seen in photo emissions and electromagnetic fields – may have an ability to harness quantum energy.

LEARNING

Suspending social structures allows for potential to go beyond them.

Past patterns become available for examination.

Experiential learning encompasses the whole person.

There are different ways of knowing beyond the intellectual.

Every learner is unique.

Meaning making and learning may be the same thing.

There is only the living moment.

Seemingly small incidents can lead to huge subjective insights.

MEANING

Reality is conferred.

Disease is making sense of our experience.

Our feelings do not live in a different world from our cells.

People seek meaning for their own lives.

People confer meaning on their experience and this determines their lives – this is interpreted through their bodily senses.

Time may be a container of meaning rather than a finite resource. How adept am I at imbuing my time with significance that reflects my personal values and identity?

Work-life balance may be experienced as out of balance when activities do not affirm the self-concept.

TIME

Time is a construct we live into as though real and it defines many of our expectations.

Time may be a container of meaning rather than a finite resource.

RELATIONSHIP

Relationship is the connectedness of all life.

With the horse, the relationship has to be embodied.

Trust is fundamental to relationship.

Force or fear constrains possibilities in the relationship.

Relationship with self – paying attention to one's own sensory experience as valid.

Relationship takes place in the articulation of the conversation and involves the emotions and feelings and bodily gestures. It is dynamic.

CONVERSATION

The act of conversation is the articulation of the relationship with self and others. Expression is literal. Whatever is held back remains in the body.

The voice is an expression of energy, much more than just the words.

Speaking aloud and thinking have very different effects in the energy field.

There are many aspects to the same conversation.

MIND-BODY INTEGRATION

The mind-body connection is absolute.

The power of affirmations to change possibilities. The power of belief as access to healing.

Our bodies advertise our beliefs and attitudes in their postures and movements. In body-work therapies, the body learns before the intellect. Real change is not embedded until it is embodied – this is the point of transformation.

COMMUNICATION

There are many levels of communication, beyond that of language, spoken or written. Communication is possible through pure thought and feelings, a sixth sense accessible through meditative states, through visualization, attitude and energy.

HORSEMANSHIP

The horse communicates through body language.

It picks up signals from the thought energy field and minute changes in the body.

It detects congruence and incongruence in the energy field.

The horse is looking for a leader it can respect.

The horse requires a relationship that is authentic.

It requires a high degree of trust.

The relationship takes time to build.

Horses are herd animals with a well-defined social hierarchy and communication system.

So many strands, so many ideas. As I followed my trail, author after author, almost feeling intuitively how one set of ideas from one area interfaced with another set of ideas in another area. Then the authors started to turn up in each other's books. And all the while thinking, processing and reflecting.

What did all this mean to me as I tried to figure out what was happening that day in the ménage, my own experience? What I was sure of, however, was that most of what I read was not known of in my organizational context – there was little or no awareness of these dynamics of human life, and certainly no understanding as to what to do about them.

As I worked my way through all this I realized that even I would not be able to complete my doctorate and write a book on top of my job. I determined that I would somehow or other need to create some time for myself. My company had developed and launched a number of family-friendly policies, one of these being a policy on sabbaticals. I proposed to my boss and my team that I would take a sabbatical of three to four months to complete my work. I talked about this with my boss and began to bring it into reality. I was to take a break from February to June the following year.

Monday 27 January 2003

I am filled with such a strong sense of my destiny. I don't exactly know how to articulate it or even how it will be fully manifest. It is as though I just know it on a deep subconscious level. And yet at the same time I feel trepidation, a little afraid. Will I be enough for it? Is it for me to take this on? Am I the one to do this, whatever it is?

This paradox is both freedom and restriction – is this the strategic space?

I now know that I am everything, all potentiality and possibility, and that everything I see is a reflection of myself.

As I watch David Whyte on the tape I am struck by his ability to be himself, and it is absolutely hypnotic and irresistible. I know now that I must leave this business – and I will only know who I am to become next as I enter that space. It does not mean that I cannot be nervous or question – but it is where my destiny must lead… it has to be me. I have to come out from behind myself.

At this time I must trust in myself and trust in the world, the universe to provide its answers. I am trying to figure too much out, instead of just allowing, releasing.

As I continued my Action Learning my deeper "why" began to emerge.

The kind of leadership that is me, that is who I am, does not exist in the modern corporation. There is no model for me to follow. No coat that fits.

And for so long I tried to be a woman that was as good as "a man" in leadership terms, what I perceived to be the leadership model, lead the way he leads, laugh at the things he laughs at, belong in the way he belongs – because when you are the only woman your need to belong is so strong that you sacrifice large parts of yourself. But that was never going to be sustainable. And the paradox was, they needed me to be me, that's why I was there.

If my organization already had what I had to bring there would be no point in me being there. There would be no struggle and therefore no growth for me.

LESSONS I HAVE LEARNED

Aligning my outer life and experiences with my inner compass creates a relentless energy.

Dig for the deeper "why". A deep "why" pulls me forward. No one else may understand it.

Follow my intuition; my unique question means that there will be a unique answer, the only guidance system I can follow is my instinct – and it is way ahead of my intellect.

PRINCIPLES TO LIVE BY

Take steps to align your inside world and your outside world.

Find the deeper "why".

Follow your instinct in investigating a question – go to the most unlikely places.

FOR LIFE IN ORGANIZATIONS

Encourage people in your organization to seek their own "whys", and understand how these relate to the business.

Does your vision/mission have a deep "why" that creates real, uncontainable emotion in all your employees? If you have to say "But wait until I explain, then you'll understand", you have some more work to do.

Many companies describe the kind of learning I am talking about as "Personal Development" and see it as doing the employees a favour or as somehow being separate from "the business". *The employee is the business –* their every thought, their every word constructs "the business". If you can expand their capacity to think, their capacity to grow, you will create new answers in your organization. And it's all personal.

EXPANDING YOUR CAPACITY TO LEARN...

Find a book, an article, something from a newspaper, a magazine – anything. But make sure it is something that you are intrigued by, interested in or curious about. As you read your piece, underline anything (yes write on it – only if it's yours, of course) that takes your interest, that "speaks" to you, like when you see something you have always known but never heard expressed. Don't think about it too much, just allow it to happen.

When you have finished, go back and review what you have underlined.

Now take a page in your journal and write what it meant to you – what the article was saying, why it was significant to you, what you learned and, most critically, what you are going to do with what you now know.

Again, this may be obvious, but you are helping your brain process and connect different pieces of information in order that a new map, a new thought, can be created. Otherwise, what you read can just disappear into the mass of information that tumbles into our everyday experience. Your brain needs to navigate. And you need to listen and allow, to see where it takes you.

Leading Yourself

You are in charge of your universe, you really are! You literally make it up. Can you believe that?

We are talking to ourselves all the time – outside – inside. What are we saying and how are we making it come true? Notice how we seek the slightest signal that what we are trying might not be working, find it immediately and give up. "I knew that would never work" – there you go! Again the horse knows what you are saying. It feels it in your energy and it senses the minute changes within your body as your muscles and tissues respond to the signal that you have just sent them. It knows before you do! Finding this out in such an undeniable way means that you get to say something different, and guess what? You get a different outcome.

I wanted to continue to do more work with horses, but how to move forward? Perry had started some horse work with a colleague, so that was a possibility. Mark wasn't an option and Peter, whilst he was an amazing rider and trainer, had never really done this kind of work before. Doing it on my own was not an option, I didn't have horses, I didn't feel confident enough, and I didn't want to do it on my own – what fun was that going to be?

I decided that I would introduce John to Peter (of the fairytale stallion) and see where we went from there. John would know.

I can't say they hit it off at first meeting but they liked each other well enough. The great opportunity here was that John and I would be able to create the workshop in a way that was completely congruent with our own approach to learning. This workshop would be about learning and not about horses, even though the horses would play a pivotal role. And we would process, process, process.

We set up some dates. We called the programme "Accelerating the Capacity to Learn" and we created a design that brought together our beliefs about people, about learning, about leadership and life. It wasn't so much about the horses, it was about learning, the horses were important – but they were not the point of the exercise.

When I say we had a design I mean we had some rough ideas of the kind of experience that we hoped our people would have, but it wasn't an exact thing, it was a "Let's go with what turns up" kind of approach supported by some questions. We had no stuff to give out. No model. No PowerPoint presentation, no manual, not even an overhead projector or a hand-out!

On the morning of the programme I got to the hotel early to discover the room laid out like a boardroom with a huge table covered in green felt, with pads and place names and all the paraphernalia that goes with that. I freaked. This was my first workshop. I was leading and it was messed up before we had even started! I was not in a good state and John was nowhere to be seen. Anyway, three or four hotel people came and cleared the table away, so we had a circle of chairs and a couple of flipcharts. I began to calm down. John arrived. People began to arrive. This was a wonderful group of people because they had all wanted to come – they had asked. They had not been requisitioned. One of the things I have learned is the importance of choosing to be there.

We all began to talk in the circle. Who we were, why we were there, what we pay attention to in our lives and where that gets us… very quickly we were in open territory, the edge of what we knew, but it wasn't scary, it was OK to be there.

We went to work with the horses, and I caught myself worrying for Peter and his team – would they be alright, would the delegates get what they needed, would they learn something? I jumped in here and there, sometimes I was needed, other times I just needed to back off, trust them to get on with it.

At the end of that first session with the horses we grouped together in the middle of the arena and in a sentence each individual expressed what they had learned. And it was all there, insight after insight, new possibility after new possibility, how they had been holding themselves back. Emotional tension hung in the air, but it was the emotion of support, acknowledgement, the kind of emotion that we had in my team meetings. John and I were the last to leave the arena, as we walked to the exit he looked at me and I looked at him with incredulity on our faces – how was this happening? We didn't seem to be *doing* anything, but all this magic was going on!

As part of the day we created a lot of time for individual reflection. I wrote in my notebook:

What I am staggered by is the depth and breadth of each human story – it's like the tip of the iceberg of so many other stories and lifetimes.

When someone speaks from their heart the hairs on the back of my neck stand up, my whole body resonates with their energy release. Still, there is so much holding back – splitting of the personality – the "work me", the "home me".

Someone said, "Why should I go home some days feeling like I never want to go back? Why do I have to hide parts of myself, presenting parts of myself that I know will be acceptable?" Where does the other stuff go? It's still present in the body.

In 45 minutes there is a space of timelessness, of not rushing, of not sticking to the clock. There is a time to speak what needs to be spoken – what there is energy for. What is present.

Someone else said, "I am changing, in these last few weeks – I want to prove that an old dog can learn new tricks."

I did not realize the power of holding the space.

When the agenda is open we cannot help but fill it with truth.

At the end of the two days we asked people to send us some thoughts, something from their book perhaps, something that they had learned.

I called in to see Peter, who was anxiously waiting to hear what had happened. I told him that after the programme had finished I had asked the delegates if they wanted to see a short video that showed what he and the team did with the horses in one of the shows.

Everyone gave an enthusiastic "Yes" and sat down again. The video demonstrated the magic between human and horse, the relationship, the leadership, the communication. You could have heard a pin drop as these individuals stared, hypnotized by the beauty of the horses that they had only been working with a few hours before. When the video finished there was just silence and a deep, humbling understanding about what they had been doing and what was possible. As I told Peter this we both ended up in tears. For me it was the release and realization of what we had done.

In a few days we had pages of email about what people had taken from the two days – the learning that they had generated, that they owned and were taking forward into their lives because it was integrated into who they were becoming.

John and I were stunned. We did not really know what we were doing or how this was happening but we knew it was something about the space we held between us, the relationship we had, the principles that we shared. And it was very, very special.

LEADERSHIP IN LEARNING – ACCELERATING THE CAPACITY TO LEARN

What a different learning experience the "Leadership in Learning" course was. There was no rigid agenda, no flipcharts, no slides, no charts or facts and figures, just people, lots of thinking and lots of enthusiasm – and it was a really refreshing and rewarding change.

There was initially some uncertainty around the direction of the two days as the style of learning was new, but people soon realized that we, the delegates, were steering the experience and in control of the direction it was going. The facilitators weren't trainers, there to "teach" us things, but were there to prompt our thinking and encourage us to go with the flow of our conversations. It was important to learn to build trust in a new group of people, as this was vital in what developed into a very personal learning experience.

On reflection, the two days for me were about making decisions and the realization that this can be a barrier to learning in itself if you are being influenced and at times delayed by an internal dialogue of self-doubt, self-confidence and risk assessment. A realization that hesitation can sometimes lead to a decision being taken out of your hands or to someone else taking control (in my case a horse running off across an arena because I had a split second's doubt about my ability!)

The decision: I can do this vs I can't do this/I will do this vs I won't do this. It's about choice.

Having looked back through my notes a few days later I was surprised not only by what I had captured but also by just how much I had written, and therefore had learnt. This has turned out to be even more than I was probably aware of at the time.

EXPERIENCE WITH THE HORSES

I was fearful of horses, not having spent any time with them before. Although the two days were not about the horses themselves, for me it was a personal challenge in the sense that I had to overcome a fear of something, which was proving to be a barrier to my learning. I found it very interesting to be able to relate my experience with the horses back to people:

My Experience of the Horses	*Reality back in the Workplace*
The horses were different on the second day, more confident and testing the boundaries or perhaps just in a "different mood".	*People sometimes "test the boundaries" and people's moods change from day to day. What works when interacting with a person or situation one day may not the next.*
The relationship was based on trust, respect and clear direction.	*All key things in a strong working relationship. Relationships need to be a two-way thing.*
The importance of non-verbal communication and the impact of	*Some people are very aware of body language and read the*

body language, eg the horse seemed to be picking up on my nervousness displayed through my body language.	*non-verbal signs. It highlighted the importance of body language as part of conveying a message or communicating.*
Getting the horse to move backwards. The need for strong, assertive behaviour.	*Again, the effect of body language when interacting with people and the need for assertive behaviour in some situations. Also the need for self-confidence.*
Rewarding the horse with a pat on the back for achieving the task.	*The importance of reward and recognition of good performance and of clear feedback or direction if something needs to change.*
Horse treading on my foot. This was a knock to my confidence.	*Never give up. Determination and confidence to face the situation and resolve it.*

It is difficult to capture all of my learning, but these are some of the key things I took away with me:

The importance of positive thinking – "I can do this…" rather than "But what about..?"

The importance of being assertive – being calm but confident in your approach to people and actions.

The need to be clear in the message or direction you are giving.

Not to be overpowered or over-influenced by any internal voice of doubt – self-confidence.

Assessing risk – what's the worst thing that can happen?

The realization that everything we do is a learning experience. If something doesn't go to plan take some learning from it and move forward.

Not to see a minor setback as failure – look at what has been achieved.

Fear is not negative, it's how you approach it – see it as an opportunity.

Conversation is about engaging or connecting with the person you are interacting with and building a relationship of trust and respect.

Communication is not just about what you say but also how you say it, eg body language, eye contact (non-verbal communication).

The importance of not being lead by others, of standing by your views.

The importance of encouragement and recognition – when the horse stepped on my foot it knocked my confidence, but the support of colleagues around me and the encouragement I received when I got back in there and achieved what I wanted to achieve made all the difference.

Anything is possible with the right mindset. The only barrier to achievement is yourself.

The first thing I noticed (not working with the horses at this stage) was the complete and utter honesty of the group I was working with on Day One. How much pain had been experienced yet each person has taken control and made something positive from this. This was my starter for 10.

Equally again, with a different group on Day Two, the honesty and sheer emotion that each person released astounded me in the morning sessions at the hotel. We all knew that we must establish trust within each group, and we most certainly did this instantly.

As an individual, I have always needed to feel as though I can trust – I guess I feel safer that way and more relaxed. If I don't achieve this feeling I just know for certain that each of us will not get the best from one another. (The horses proved to me the truth of this).

Certainly since the session my group on Day Two have all spoken separately, and I really believe we have bonded in some way. We are still all checking each other out to see if there is anything each of us can do to support the group. This has never happened to me before when attending a learning session. We have achieved trust.

I also saw that how you behave with people works the same way with horses; if it does that with horses it must be so essential to behave. When I say behave I mean disciplinary issues, gaining respect, manners, conversations etc.

I had done this when bringing up my children but I suppose to a certain extent

I felt that I had done my bit because… yes it took a lot of effort, devotion and time, and I guess I thought that was part of my past life. I realized it wasn't, I needed to put in effort, every day, devotion every day, and to achieve all this would take an awful lot of time and effort. However, it is necessary to achieve the result I require. The time spent with the horses spelt this out to me.

I also learnt that consistency is important within myself. I must work on staying cool and calm … it does make sense... if I become irate where will it get me? I know the horses would have thought me a fool to behave in such a way. Keeping calm allows thinking time, reshaping time, problem-solving time.

On Day Two my horse was quite spirited, I had to work on these things – he was testing me out that's for sure. I realized that I must never give up. I can overcome.

I won't ever forget making the horse walk backwards – without ever touching or pushing him. This was an important achievement for me – the horse only responded when I held my head up high and showed my determination.

So, again, approach things differently, have confidence to carry things out. Some people appear to have a gift for putting others down, and when this happens I will always relate to my own moment on that special day. My reaction will be so different.

Both horses I worked with showed me loyalty, they awaited my directives, my encouragement and my strength. From a leadership perspective it showed me that I can still go further with anything I do, I can move on, I can overcome. Issues can be solved in some way. My strengths cannot only help me, I can also help others. In turn, others may hopefully become happier, stronger, more decisive people themselves.

One thing has just sprung into my mind, and this was to do with the horse I worked with on Day Two. He just would not lift any of his legs – something I had achieved so easily on Day One with another horse. I thought I had exhausted everything, but when I decided physically to push his huge body away from me with my body weight he gave in – he said "Fine, I will do this for you. You really mean this. I am not going to fight you any more!" I knew then that you need to convince people 100% – and that 50% is just not enough. Also, some people require more negotiation than others. Ginger was no pushover.

Finally, the energy I found within myself when I ran with the horse – it just oozed out of me, and I kept this energy for ages. I felt totally rejuvenated, re-motivated … just so full of life. It did show me something about unlimited energy which when I feel tired and ready to flop I will hopefully be able to draw upon because I have proved it is there, and will always be there for me to access.

I am so glad I had this opportunity to come along. It's an experience everyone needs to have.

I needed some time to soak and reflect on what the course had taught me before giving feedback. Here goes:

The course agenda was interesting in that it allowed ample time to think. Normally you are given a set task to complete within "tight" timescales. The technique of having no fixed agenda worked well as everyone felt they were given time to express their thoughts. Having time to think was great – I would come up with my "answers" in five minutes, as I have been "programmed" to work, then my mind would drift on to other things or wider subjects. I was thinking that I didn't have anything else to add and was almost waiting to be called back to the group but every time something else came through that added to what I had already put down. This time to think made me realize that I was using my brain more, or perhaps in a different way. I had discovered new mental muscles!

Life story – a very interesting reflective process of writing down and communicating your life story to someone else. It really makes you see what is important to you, what you want to tell people about yourself, and maybe what you don't want to tell, which is also revealing. I am currently writing my "Life CV"; this is something that I thought about before the course but now is even more useful. This CV will contain my achievements outside of work, the milestones etc. I will use it to remind myself what I have done in my life – that can be a great motivator.

Childhood dream/love – this came through to me in a flash during the course as Alison asked some questions. It was weird, like my life flashing before me. I could see how that childhood love had influenced me all the way through. The hard bit is how do I use that "love" to do "what I really want to do". I need to work on this.

Dream – the process of visualizing a dream or goal was also very powerful. Taking it to the extreme and then back again had the effect of making the dream not such a big challenge after all. My dream was about publicizing a band that I have followed for 14 years to give them continued success so that I can continue to enjoy their music. Since the course I have got approval from the editor to put a self-financed promo CD on the cover of an independent rock magazine with a circulation of 1,000. I have also been in communication with the band members who responded that it "sounds interesting" and have given me their contact number. We are currently working on sorting out the copyright issues before the August edition. Nothing is impossible.

In terms of my job, the course reinforced that emotions are the key to behaviours and this ties in very strongly to the behavioural safety work I am doing. To date, year on year, the Manufacturing team have achieved a 48% reduction in "lost time" accidents, a 62% reduction in reportable lost time accidents and an 83% reduction in total days lost. Just think what we could do if we were really trying! This is real money saved through not covering lost time and ultimately saving on our insurance premium. I have booked myself on a night class course for A/S level psychology to further my understanding of human behaviour and we will be rolling out a behavioural safety course at Magor next year.

Horses – taught me about focusing on a goal, confident body language and just going for it. This is applicable in my role and I am using this approach in some areas. Interestingly enough I have also used the horse techniques on our two-year old gelding and he is enjoying walking backwards. I have made several horses at our stables walk backwards, even a nasty loner who tried to intimidate me in the field. This is much to the amazement of the "horsey set" and I am now revered as some sort of Monty Roberts, the famous horse-whisperer. I think they all want me to train their horses now!!

Dreams are often postponed or completely forgotten because of the people around us telling us that it can't be done, or flagging up the problems that will be encountered. Better still, we start putting up the brick walls in our own heads... I personally think that the negativity of the world can sometimes rub off into our own lives, and unless we take time out to think in depth about things we don't see the external and internal influences... for some people they won't see unless they are led or shown the way...

Our group was very open and positive and we were willing to listen to one another. We were given the freedom on the course to explore and learn from each other at a pace that was comfortable. I said at the time that I wondered how different the atmosphere on the course would be if there was someone present who was cynical or didn't want to be there...

Since being on the course and speaking to account managers I have been amazed at the level of cynicism, which makes me wonder how open people are to learning or trying something new.

The past does not need to be the future (old ways aren't always the best and new ways may not be either, but if we don't give them a go how can we ever really tell?)

Everyone has the potential to change (though the choice must be from the individual themselves).

Mind, heart and spirit. (By aligning the three into what you are trying to achieve ensures focus; when the body has had enough the mind will keep you stimulated, when the mind has had enough your spirit will lift you high and encourage you on – if what you are doing is at your core being, the heart of you.)

Possibilities not probabilities (focusing on what you can do and not what you cannot do).

WORKING WITH THE HORSES

Clarity around what it is you are trying to do – clear, specific instructions. At work we assume that we communicate clearly; this isn't always the case. You must have clarity in your own mind before expecting others to understand what it is you are trying to achieve; this reduces confusion and ensures that you all work towards the same goal.

Working together in unity. The process is much simpler and takes a lot less time and energy if you work together to achieve the goal.

Relax. Be aware of how you may be coming across when speaking to another person – body language, posture, facial expression, tone, heartbeat. This may be the deciding factor whether a person assists or rejects what it is you are asking them to do...

Encouragement – body language may give away how you are feeling, eg if a person is laid back and fairly unenthusiastic when asking someone to do something, the person they are asking may mirror the behaviour.

Compare that approach to a person who stands upright, is confident and enthusiastic – compare the response.

Approach to task – there isn't always one way to do something. Just because it works well for somebody else doesn't mean the same approach will work well for you. If it works well for you use it!

If you are going to compare your technique to somebody else's, remember your way isn't always going to be wrong.

Being able to try different options and picking the one that works best for the person.

Freedom – boundaries are in place but there is also the freedom to learn, re-access and express/talk things through. With this comes an element of risk; if you are not a natural risk-taker you need to understand that it is OK and that things may not be as bad as you think they are going to be, even if something does go wrong.

EXTRAS FROM DAY ONE

People/animals feel your emotions – positive or negative.

You need to develop a level of trust with a horse, it's about partnership/relationship. If you can build a relationship with a horse why should a person be any different?

You can't get a horse to do something it doesn't understand – it's about clarity, understanding and focus.

Share ideas, don't internalize everything.

It is easier to work alongside like-minded individuals.

FEAR can make you stumble and destroy your dreams.

Conversation and communication can bring people together or cause division.

STEPPING OUT

The fear of the lake stops the deer saving its own life...

The lake in my mind represents the unknown, the risk factor, the possibilities clouded by the "what ifs" and a lot of missed opportunities in life.

Sometimes a little too much thought before the action stage. PACE increase.

The perfectionist in me, the deep thinking and reflection.

Internal dialogue without expression – too many unanswered questions.

Trust is key in all relationships that I have. Working with the horses highlighted something that I have not been aware of. Having built the trust with the horse, I let my guard down and didn't consider the risks that may arise. At work, risk is something I give consideration to, in relationships with people I thought I did the same; what I didn't realize was that once the trust is built I lose sight of the opportunity for risk. Now what happened with the horse next was unexpected because we had been working well together – whether it felt my excitement and became excited itself or whether it was testing me I don't know. It didn't rear but to a short person like myself when a horse stops out of the blue and yanks its head right back it knocks you for six and lifts you off your feet. The body reacts – your eyes feel like they've popped out of your head, your legs shake and feel like they are going to give way, your heartbeat accelerates. The inner voice says "Keep calm, relax, slow your heartbeat down" and the outer voice says "Don't let go of the rope, soothe the horse verbally and physically". The fear of what could happen had happened and you are left with two choices: 1) Panic and walk away, or 2) Confront the fear, learn from it and prepare yourself in the event of another risk.

Get back into the situation and get on with it. After a few circuits and feeling relaxed it happened again, but with twice the force. This time something strange happened, I heard myself say aloud to the horse "No, I don't think so." His behaviour wasn't acceptable and I found myself telling him so.

With the horse I chose not to bear a grudge and try again. With people I looked at how I would react and found that I have less tolerance.

If a trust is broken or something happens just the once this may not have enough impact to make me change my perception of the person, but if it happens again then for me that relationship at work is over. I re-establish the boundaries; let them know that their behaviour is unacceptable. However, from thereon the relationship is guarded and the freedom has gone.

Sometimes the thought of the fear is worse than the fear itself…

What you can see and hear in these words is real. It is not about what activity the course participants engaged in with the horse, lifting its foot or leading it or running with it... what was important was the mirror that the horse holds up to each and every person, reflecting back their own unique embodied self – conscious and unconscious – for inquiry and movement. Every learning agenda individually catered for, personalized and, most importantly, owned by the individual, to be carried forward in their lives.

LESSONS I HAVE LEARNED

As I trust myself, so I must offer others that trust in themselves.

People are amazing – again!

Everyone will learn what they need to learn, if they are just given a safe, unconditional space to do it in.

Even in an open workshop such as these, what is shared is still only the very tip of the iceberg. There is much, much more.

People have their own answers, perfect and complete for them.

Real learning is the engagement of the whole living being – mind, body, soul engaging in something of deep importance to us. It involves a willingness to suspend our beliefs and open ourselves to a new sensory experience. It requires a desire to absorb a possible change as a better option than the current scenario.

PRINCIPLES TO LIVE BY

Trust yourself.

Inquire into everything – every gesture, every sound, every breath is made for a reason.

The body, the voice and the energy field.

FOR LIFE IN ORGANIZATIONS

Just occasionally tear up the agenda, dump the presentations, unplug the Proxima, take away the tables, sit a circle and see what turns up.

EXPANDING YOUR CAPACITY TO LEARN...

Get into your body. If you do not already do some kind of activity, do something. I would recommend anything like the Alexander Technique, yoga, dance, Rolfing, Hellerwork, horse-riding, sport of any kind, singing. Something that brings you into an awareness of your body, how you use it, and what tension might be there. Our mind and body are not separate. It is through your body senses that you experience the world, all in the same living moment. If you already participate in some form of activity, become more aware of what you are experiencing when you are doing it.

And then, guess what? Yes, write about your experiences – explore the experiences and your learning through your body.

Who Are You Becoming?

Is your future history based on your past experience? Is this it? How many more possibilities could there be for you if you knew you were in charge of your universe?

Working developmentally with the horse provides a completely unique gateway to human potential, transformational learning and leadership capability. The experience of having a creature of such grace, beauty, power and sheer life choose to be with you and follow you is truly life changing.

It is life changing because to create that connection you have had to look into yourself to find something not only for the horse but also for yourself. In that moment the genie is out of the bottle. This is not a one-time offer. You get to go back – again and again, to the edge of your potential, and reinvent it over and over.

The whole world has changed and nothing and no one will ever stop you again!

A few weeks later my boss called me to a meeting – very mysterious – one of those "something's going on but I will have to kill you if I tell you" meetings. He explained that there were going to be a number of changes in the business in the coming year and that one of those was that he would be retiring.

We had talked previously of my plans to set up my own business in a year or two (you know, far enough off not to worry), once I had completed my doctorate and book – all very rational and logical.

But life does not often work in this way.

He suggested that, since he was retiring, it might be best to move into my own business sooner rather than later. I was to think about things over the next couple of weeks. As often happened in these kinds of meetings my brain began to slow up its processing speed – what did all this mean exactly? Like how soon? Like – Oh no, am I ready for this? You better be – you asked for it! Ever heard of the expression "rubber meeting the road"? Just act normal!!

This trusting in the universe thing was getting a bit out of control!

As I left the meeting and began to contemplate what we had talked about, there was really no decision to be made, it had already been made, it was just turning up. This was not the moment of decision; that had been reached a long time ago.

Wednesday 1 February 2003

Things are moving quickly now. I am facing the leap now.

…Will I be OK, cast adrift from the corporate safety net? I mean, I know I will, but I do have a few little doubts, I don't even want to give them airtime.

One day, one moment at a time… pickin' daisies… only one life, only the soul's journey – go to the scary places – that's where life is – everything else is adverts!

I am becoming intolerant of the TV, the media, the "ideas culture" that it is assumed I live within. There are large chunks of it that I do not subscribe to, have never subscribed to, and it's starting to really annoy me!

I continued my work in the business. This was very important to me. This was not just a job to be dropped, to be moved on from – this struggle had been my life for the last five years or so – inside and outside – and without it I would not have become who I am becoming. The people I had worked with were not their job titles or boxes on structure charts – they were real people, real relationships, and emotional relationships. They mattered to me, as I mattered to them.

It was the relationships between us that enabled us to grow and stretch and learn; to not be afraid because there was a special place that we could go where no matter what we would be OK, we would be accepted and we would not be judged.

This was the space I had created out of my team meetings – people and their dreams came first, where that fitted into the business came second. This way you worked with energy and possibility not drudgery and probability!

When you believe in people, sometimes more than they believe in themselves, they can do miracles. And as I became more of who I really was, each of them did too. I never hid my fear, my joy, my humour, my sadness, my struggle and my doubts, and so it was a very human place that recognized and celebrated every small step that any one of us ever made. There was always a lot of emotion in our team meetings. These people were a part of me and now it was time to go.

I began to realize that, in a sense, it was time to go because the struggle was reaching closure – it was time for a new chapter, in all our lives.

It was all settled. I would leave the business in a couple of months, but would continue to consult for a year or for as long as was necessary. However, it was to be a number of weeks before I could tell my team.

Another workshop and the essence of this work continued to coalesce in my mind:

Where do my thoughts come from?
   Who is the witness?
   Who is it that experiences the story?
   The me that is the same me as when I was 5, 6, 7, 27 or 37?
   All there has been is expansion and unfolding – being able to trust myself to utter into the universe the secrets of my innermost thoughts. Because they come from somewhere – they are not to be denied. In denying them, I deny myself. I deny my future possibilities, I deny the future unfolding, I deny the attainment of congruence and I deny this, my gift, myself, to others.
   Where do my thoughts come from?

They come from my body, my awareness. The head stuff, it's just a translation of knowledge, an interpretation that does not even carry the full representation of the knowledge, the thing itself. Because it is the body that knows first – this is where intuition, instinct and emotions lie – the body knows. The body, my body, senses the slightest touch, the fluctuation in the energy field. My body and its energy field and its physical sensations are ahead of me – and they are truth – the intellect comes in to translate it with rules and socialization and all the conditioning, but if you took all that away, my body knows.

I have to learn to listen, to listen and hear what I am struggling to tell myself – the inner me, the witness who is seeking to expand and integrate and believe in herself, that what she truly thinks and feels is valid, no matter what everyone else thinks or what she imagines in advance others might think.

The emotions are what we pay attention to – there is more congruence and authenticity, and to human beings this is irresistible.

I am sensing more and more that it is in the emotional, energetic layer that wisdom and knowledge truly exists. The intellect is just another level – not so deep or so rich.

This process is about awareness. Bringing what is out of awareness into awareness, into consciousness – and out of this comes the capacity to learn, the energy to act and the courage to lead.

As you open the valve of awareness, insights stream in from everywhere – and you don't know which skill, which relationship, which project they will affect – possibly everything.

What is the relationship between awareness and energy?

Awareness is the navigator.

Determining what I notice, what I pay attention to.

As the awareness is expanded the subconscious patterns of our lives come into view – now seen, they can be shifted, and as they fall away the energy begins to pour out, it begins to flow and expand.

It takes energy to hold the subconscious patterns in place, and when they are released there is flow. And all within the behest of the individual – enabling them to do this for themselves.

As the sense of purpose comes to life and struggles to break free from its previous constraints, the energy flows into the unified field and literally brings forth the future, sending waves out, creating reality…

The time came to tell my team. I met John the night before our team meeting to discuss my plans.

Tuesday 25 March 2003

Every now and then life offers you moments that are real; they are pure magic – transcendent wonder. Today I had such a moment – and the thing about these moments is that they come upon you so surprisingly. I met with John to tell him I was leaving and moving on to pastures new – to my dream of The Centre for Natural Leadership.

I hadn't planned what I was going to say – I didn't realize it would be so hard – he felt something, showed something, it meant something. It wasn't just an "Oh that's a pity, what are you going to do?" conversation; it was real, as it has always been with us.

He talked of the space I create for people – he talked of the last workshop we did and how special it was, he talked of the space I give him and the elemental waters he saw in me that day. He talked of how close he is to me – and when he asked me what I thought the team's reaction would be tomorrow tears welled up from nowhere and he held my hand.

Working with this group of people has been a special moment in time for me. I found myself looking forward to the day of our meetings. They have helped me become who I am today – and it's such a gift – it's like I gave it to others and I got it right back.

John made me feel… what? Special, I guess, unique – me – just me – and it's enough. There was a bubble around us. I did not want to leave, to break the space – neither did he – because after that moment a new era would begin. These are the moments of life…

A few days later John called to say that he had been thinking about our team meeting last week and that at the time he had just wanted to get on with things. He had not seen the poignancy of it, how pivotal it was that the dream was coming to fruition and he now had a sense of the gap that I would leave

– the depth of feeling, of authenticity, of inspiration – and he had a feeling that the bosses did not even realize how great a gap I would leave.

The gap is so much more than the words and the projects – it's an essence, a being, a conversation, a possibility, a space...

LESSONS I HAVE LEARNED...

Just take one step and then the next – hold the intention, but don't anticipate every eventuality, trust and allow.

I realize that, through my journal, I have been "Action Learning" all my life. I have been processing and learning and reflecting all along. It was so ordinary to me, I did not even notice.

When I ride Henry I have to be so focused that the hour flies in a minute – it is completely timeless, it's like meditation. Every time he offers me an edge, every time there is so much to learn, I cannot hold on to it all, many times I am physically afraid. Why on earth do I do this? I feel like I will never be able to ride. There was a moment when I thought I would give up my dream, because it frightened me so much and I thought – Who am I kidding? Then Peter said to me, "You have to take a lifetime to learn to ride – just like the rest of us."

PRINCIPLES TO LIVE BY...

Determine who you are already and who you are going to become, and talk yourself into that reality, you are the big star in your own production, everyone else is a bit player – may as well have it the way you want it.

Take the smallest step every day towards your dreams.

Think, learn, bring forth your future, and do not trust it to the fleeting thoughts that flit through your mind every instant of the day.

FOR LIFE IN ORGANIZATIONS...

Are the people in your organization alive?

Is there fun and laughter in the work?

Are the people learning? Do they look forward to their "performance reviews" knowing that they will be recognized and inspired? Will it be a deep conversation about their loves, their ideas and their dreams? Will it be a conversation that they will leave with more energy than they arrived?

Imagine if this were the case.

I think there is a new model for the role of Human Resources management in organizations today. There is a new paradigm emerging that has to be about energy – finding it, nurturing it, fanning the faintest glow of a charcoaled ember, feeding it – not measuring it against some historic competency framework but against the diverse individual talents and dreams of the people that make up the group.

Align the inside and the outside. This will take belief, faith and courage and there will be no flag flying for a long time – but there you go – the leadership space.

ENHANCING YOUR CAPACITY TO LEAD...

I want to share a poem with you, a poem written by Dawna Markova. It is a poem I have recited many times in the workshops that I have run. It speaks to me very deeply of the greatest tragedy there is…

I Will Not Die An Unlived Life

I will not die an unlived life
I will not live in fear of falling
Or catching fire.
I choose to inhabit my days,
To allow my living to open me
To make me less afraid,
More accessible,
To loosen my heart
Until it becomes a wing,
A torch, a promise.

I choose to risk my significance;
To live
So that which came to me as seed
Goes to the next as blossom
And that which came to me
As blossom
Goes on as fruit.

Leading in the World

Having had the experience with the horse and faced all the implications that it offers, the world is then your own. If you can move a horse from 15 feet away from you with the power of your own mind, what can't you do?

Here is the gateway, the living gateway into the leadership of yourself, the most powerful place you can be. All you have to do is believe, go to the edge and fly.

It was a couple of months before I would leave my business, this place that in the beginning had seemed so alien to me, in which I had struggled to find my place. And even during this time there was so much to learn.

It was so ironic that, now things were going so well, it was time to go. At a management group meeting, that I didn't attend, my managing director acknowledged my work with a set of medals from the Commonwealth Games. He said that they owed me a debt of gratitude, that I had put learning at the heart of the business, that everywhere you looked in our business there was learning happening; he laughed and admitted that sometimes he needed a translator, but that it was worth it in the end. The words meant all the more to me because I had not been there and they had been reported to me – he had not had to say these words but he had. Like I said, the cheering usually turns up after the job of leadership has been done!

People were full of congratulations and support for me, particularly those who knew of my journey, who had been intimately involved in my journey. Some of those who knew me less well would say, "You are very brave... going off on your own". I thought this was strange! For me this was just the next step, there was no real bravery involved, that would imply that I did not believe in myself or that I was waiting for someone else to believe in me.

I had a job to do and I had to get on with it. I didn't quite know exactly what it was, but I certainly had to go and find out.

People would say to me something like, "So you are going to be a consultant..." I tried that on for size, but something inside said, "No, no, that's not it, not quite it".

I am lots of different things, expressed in lots of different ways:

I am a speaker.

I am a writer.

I am a researcher.

I am a leader.

I am a learner.

I am a change architect.

I am a mother.

I am a horse-rider.

I am a woman.

I am a part of the unified field.

I am an expression of the universe.

And all of this depends on who *you* are, because I am only one half of the conversation.

And as I began to live more into the person that I really am, I began to meet and communicate with new people, people that I can talk to on the edge of my knowing and who already understand; they don't look at me sideways and mumble under their breath. Not only do they understand but they are a step ahead of me on the path. I am not alone.

Writing this book has been an interesting experience. Again, I learned many things.

Sunday 18 May 2003

Some things I learned today.

I found the diary I lost when Alex was born – and read through some of it. I had forgotten the despair I had been through. How did I do it?

Looking back now – at the words – that time was horrendous for me. Depressed, lonely, with no sleep for months on end. It made me see my life today as a breeze, it put it in a whole different perspective.

The other remarkable thing is that everything I had ever wished for I have created – I can see the seeds of my dreams.

The other thing I learned was that I nearly missed the point of what I am doing – which is not the intellectualizing of my philosophy but its experiential living and exploration – for myself.

And I nearly bypassed my living for the doctorate, when it is all about a holistic approach to human performance. And when I consider the pressure under which I completed my Masters it all falls back into place. I am going to put my health and well-being at the centre of my philosophy – mind and body…

I have had a lovely couple of days at home, working, cocooned in my own world – reaching out when I wanted to. It's like I need these times to think deeply, to give birth to new ideas, privately. Almost to be with myself and all that I can access. See the meaning transform before my eyes as I try to get every ounce of it expressed. It's wonderful. I feel centred. I feel me…

I feel like I am stepping into the reflection of my own light – and it is dazzling. It's me, but it is more than me, it is humanity… I do believe it is my purpose to show people themselves, their own dazzling, beautiful uniqueness – irreplaceable. There is no doubt in my mind that it is in this way that the energy to heal is released, in acceptance and love. To hold up the mirror so people can see their own light and be "healed" (on whatever level) by their own brilliance.

This is my commitment to humanity and the promise of my life.

Wednesday 2 July 2003

A profound insight just launched itself into my head! I know what love is. This timeless emotion that crosses all cultures, that is the strongest and most revered of all human attributes.

The reason I began to shake uncontrollably on that first workshop was that I was being all of me – intellect, emotion and soul – I was stepping into the sheer vibrational field that is me. And just now, in the bathroom as I was brushing my teeth, I was thinking – Oh I must talk about my team meetings and how I began to bring more of me into the meetings – I waited less, and as I did all this I was me. That is where love comes from!

It's all about uncovering, and being all that you are – and the degree to which you are able to do this in any relationship will be the degree of love that you experience in that relationship. Because it's all a mirror anyway, so what comes back is self to a degree, until as you both pull back the layers there are no layers and there is connection in the universal field.

Connection – the word I have sought all my life.

I wrote, "It all comes down to love", and I was right.

Connection was about love, all along. I am breathless at this insight. It feels like a piece of gossamer, like I can glimpse it for an instant, and then it is gone. But that is why when you do what you "love" you are being "you" in such a way that the layers peel away to reveal pure truth, pure energy, pure inspiration, pure love.

That's why on the third workshop my affirmation changed. It changed from power to love and I never knew why.

So love, the ultimate force, the strongest field, means the falling away of everything else. It means authenticity, complete congruence with every fibre of being. This is why love can heal. It is the gift of self in a way, all of the self – because what use is it if it is not expressed? And it is perfect, because it is part of nature. And nature is designed in perfect balance and harmony...

As part of my research into this phenomenon I held a small research seminar, where some leading academics and learning specialists would come along and explore this work with the horses, from a human developmental perspective.

Sadhanchu Pulsale, one of the participants, wrote of his experience and shared it with the group. He said:

I was hesitant at first. I had not been this close to a big animal like this for years. Not fear, but hesitation.

I looked him in the eye. He was compassionate.

He became my guide. He helped me overcome my hesitation and I just will not

*forget the first sight – the first time I made eye contact with this beautiful animal...
and in those eyes I saw... there was a universe.*

He led me, I did not lead him.

*That was a learning point for me, I was holding the rope, but he was the one
who was leading. I had the larger neo-cortex, I was higher up the food chain, yet
he helped me connect to a more profound level. And I felt this so distinctly because
I realized that I could not lie to this animal.*

*I could fool all of you here, and maybe I have done that in the past, but there
was no way I could be inauthentic and fool him. It just doesn't work – the moment
you lie, he knows.*

*I think that is something profound, profoundly significant for all of us who
inadvertently lead lives of lies, thanks to the way the corporate world makes us
behave. That was a beautiful, moving, sense for me.*

*I am really going back with that. Apart from anything else, I just feel like
spending more time with these animals.*

You sense a real bonding here.

There was complete silence as his words hung in the air, heavy with truth.

As we continued our conversation that afternoon, reflecting
and considering our experience, the discussion took another unexpected
turn. David Rooke, another leading expert in leadership development,
said:

There is something here about being in touch with the sacred.

*You go to a meeting – you go into the room with your head down, and there's
an agenda, usually no natural light, and the removal from nature is severe. There
is nothing sacred.*

*We go into that [horse] arena, and there is dirt on the floor and... beasts, you
can't fail to notice that, and it brings alive something which would be so wonderful
to bring alive in the corporate tower.*

John said:

*It's the self-discovery... you can tell people about work-life balance or whatever it
is they want to know, but until we discover it for ourselves it is of no value.*

Hadyn said:

Because we have to be physically and emotionally involved – that is what is so powerful.

There were many insights that emerged for all of us that day. The piece of the jigsaw that seemed to fall into place for me was the idea of a "sacred space". And what I mean by that is a space where you are not interrupted by the mobile phone, an email, an unfinished project, where you are not expected to fulfil the demands of a boss, a husband, a wife, a child, or anyone else who might be running your life.

A sacred space in which to think, to reflect, to learn, to talk, to be. A sacred space in which you are fully present.

The relationship with the horse offers us such a space, to become fully present, mind and body, and for an instant we move into the centre of the living moment where we can be with ourselves and with the horse, in complete alignment and congruence, in commune with nature and the universe.

The organization is our modern-day community.

There are greater responsibilities here than the employment contract developed in the Industrial Revolution, the profit to be made and the shareholder to be satisfied.

People are aching, literally and metaphorically, for a space, a space that is worthy of their lives. A "sacred" space in which they can be who they are capable of becoming, where they can form authentic relationships that sustain and inspire them, and where they can make from these relationships the contribution that is their purpose and destiny, where they can risk themselves on the very edge of their possibilities.

It is from these spaces that the future inventions that sustain our economic prosperity will come, a new alignment of energy and resources, a new way to lead in the world, a new model of organization.

I bought Henry. Leaving my company gave me the capital I needed to buy him.

The universe provided.

Thursday 15 May 2003

Riding today – softer in the seat, blocking with the seat.

Using the ribcage. Rising with the hips.

Going forward in the dynamic dance. Not staccato – more flow – energy coming out from me. Forward, always forward – allowing the horse to flow.

I am the horse.

Using my energy.

My breathing is his breathing. Deep breaths, then I won't get tired. I'll get my second wind.

The feeling of everything disappearing; the air on my face my only awareness.

No end, just a dynamic continuation, an unfolding step by step. Using what I know to create the future I desire. Listening, trusting to my own loves, as the greatest power and contribution that I can make.

I lose my temper with my children, my house is still messy and my car has bits of toys and crisps all over the back seat. And sometimes all there is in the fridge is a pot of out-of-date Greek yogurt that Steve says I put in the trolley to look good – and he's right. And this is life.

But I am living my dreams. They seemed impossible when I looked from afar, but when the day comes it's just the next step, the next breath, as each living moment energetically follows the next.

It's funny but I do believe that the greatest gift we have is the greatest contribution we have to make, and usually it is so effortless to us that we don't notice it.

Look around you, look down; if the path you see is beautifully paved, with landscaped flowers and shrubs, and it stretches endlessly before you – beware!

This is not your path, but someone else's. Stop; listen, with every part of you, into the deafening silence of yourself and wait. There will be a voice, a vision, a sense of the step you need to make – you know already. Off the path, into the unknown, the brambles, and the uneven ground – you are a part of those brambles and that uneven ground, connected to it all.

The path is not what we see ahead, it's what we leave behind.

If you are afraid, relish it – you are alive.

When we are doing what we love, what we are meant to do, we are resonating with the universe. Our energy field is aligned and congruent, the most powerful force there is. The waves of an energy field such as this stretch forward in time, how far I do not know, because time is not the linear concept we hold it to be. The waves go forward and begin to create a pattern, a new pattern that other waves become attracted to, and a forward, dynamic flow is effortlessly created.

Leadership, true leadership, the leadership of personal destiny not positional power, is leadership of the energetic field. For there is no other that you truly lead. It's their choice to follow, and they follow because something they see, hear or feel in you is in them. In order to lead in the energetic field there must be alignment and congruence. This can only be found in the connection, understanding and manifestation of your unique purpose and contribution.

Usually, when this connection is found, this understanding is reached, the manifestation is lived, the contribution is not for yourself alone – it is for all of humanity – a cause that must be led, an idea whose time has come, a challenge that must be met. And someone has handed to you the Olympic torch, to take it forward – only you, you are the only one, which is why it has come to you. Taking this responsibility will offer you all the learning and growth you will ever need.

Funny thing is, in this responsibility you usually find freedom.

Before you think I have gone off into the realms of philosophy, I bring you back to the mirror of the horse, where alignment and congruence, vision, direction and purpose give you an instantaneous answer in real time from the energetic field.

This is real. More real than anything I know.

Use this knowledge to navigate the infinite potential of your life.

And then... be...

Further Information

Further information about The Centre for Natural Leadership can be found at learningandleadership.com.

Alison Winch can be contacted at alisonwinch@learningandleadership.com

INTRODUCTION TO THE LIFE-TIME NAVIGATOR

Unlike most "time management" systems, the Life-Time Navigator is not about time at all but is focused upon *energy and learning* resulting in self-leadership and personal fulfilment. It's about supporting you in becoming everything you want to become. It holds the human being as a living organism, a part of nature not a computer or machine. It brings alive the principle, well-known from physics and philosophy, that there is only this moment, a series of never-ending "nows", and since there is only this moment you can make many many choices as to creating your desired future.

The idea of *"energy"* is central to engaging with the Life-Time Navigator – finding it, accessing it, generating it and sustaining it. The Navigator operates in the energetic layer of your life, the place of action and movement in the world on many different levels. The place where you really already know what you want and have all the resources you need to achieve your dreams, you just need to pay attention in a new way. This is the space where personal inspiration becomes the source of real change in your life.

Your own sense of *well-being* is fundamental to the living energy available to you. The structure and functioning of our bodies influences the ideas and thoughts we are capable of having. Thinking of our bodies as living processes that produce a structure, rather than as fixed machines, allows the realization of a whole new layer of possibility for health and well-being. The Navigator seeks to promote optimal health and well-being, not just an absence of illness.

Learning and enhanced self-awareness are at the heart of this approach. Accelerating your capacity to learn each and every day will enable you to meet challenges in all areas of your life, to achieve your goals and dreams. You will become your own "life coach", learning to listen to your inner navigator.

The Life-Time Navigation system builds upon the overwhelming amount of evidence from all spheres of science that through our perceptions *we create our own worlds* and then live into our expectations as though they are reality. Taking responsibility for the world that you create means that you can change it any way you like. You can change your world, change your life, change yourself – if you so choose.

As a living being, you need not be constrained by past patterns if they no longer help you, you are *free to create new patterns* and thoughts that will take you energetically forward to everything you desire.

OVERVIEW

There are three main components to the Life-Time Navigation system – a journal, a pocket diary and the organizer itself, which contains all the sections.

THE JOURNAL

The purpose of the journal is to support you in developing your capacity for self-awareness, learning and reflection. Often through our education we are taught to absorb the thoughts and ideas of others and as children and adolescents we become unsure of our own thoughts and experiences. Using a journal or just writing a stream of thoughts offers you the opportunity to really listen to yourself, to articulate and expand what you are thinking and feeling, developing your own ideas and learning to trust yourself. Developing this kind of inner awareness is pivotal in enhancing leadership and learning capability. The journal can then be used as a resource for further understanding and growth throughout the other sections of the Life-Time Navigator.

THE POCKET DIARY

The purpose of the pocket diary is to enable you to take a look over the medium term – the next 18 months or so. There is something about holding our own physical representation of our futures in our hands, being able to turn over to each month and absorb the unique symbols, notations, letters, colours that mark this time as personally ours that registers more robustly in our brains and memories. Each month includes reminders to consider your intentions for the month, the values that you wish to live and the activities that will make you feel great – creating and sustaining your energy.

THE LIFE-TIME NAVIGATOR ORGANIZER

The Life-Time Navigator organizer is laid out in sections:
Goals and Dreams
Daily Diary
Notes and Ideas
Learning and Leadership
Inspiration
Well-Being
Energetic Leadership.

The Life-Time Navigator can be ordered from
alisonwinch@learningandleadership.com

Bibliography/Further Reading

Bateson, G, *Steps to an Ecology of Mind*. The University of Chicago Press, 1972

Bays, B, *The Journey – An Extraordinary Guide for Healing Your Life and Setting Yourself Free*. Thorsons, 1999

Belasik, P, *Riding Towards the Light – An Apprenticeship in the Art of Dressage Riding*. JA Allen & Co Ltd, 1990

Benson, H, *Timeless Healing – The Power and Biology of Belief*. Fireside, 1997

Boaz, N, *Evolving Health – The Origins of Illness and How the Modern World is Making Us Sick*. John Wiley & Sons, 2002

Bolman, LG & Deal, TE, *Leading with Soul – An Uncommon Journey of Spirit*. Jossey-Bass, 2001

Chopra, D, *Unconditional Life – Discovering the Power to FulFill Your Dreams*. Bantam Books, 1991

Cousins, N, *Anatomy of an Illness as perceived by the Patient – Reflections on Healing and Regeneration*. Bantam Books, 1979

Fisher, D, Rooke, D & Torbert, B, *Personal and Organizational Transformations Through Action Inquiry*. Edge/Work Press, 2000

Ford, D, *The Dark Side of the Light Chasers – Reclaiming your Power, Creativity, Brilliance and Dreams*. Riverhead Books, 2001

Gawani Pony Boy, *Horse Follow Closely – Native American Horsemanship*. BowTie Press, 1998

Gilpin, A, *Unstoppable People – How Ordinary People Achieve Extraordinary Things*. Random House, 1998

Gladwell, M, *The Tipping Point – How Little Things Can Make a Big Difference*. Abacus, 2002

Grandin, T, *Thinking in Pictures and Other Reports from my Life with Autism*. Vintage Books, 1996

Handy, C, *The Hungry Spirit: Beyond Capitalism – A Quest for Purpose in the Modern World*. Random House, 1997

Harri-Augstein, S & Thomas, LF, *Learning Conversations – The Self-organized Learning Way to Personal and Organizational Growth*. Routledge, 1991

Heller, J, and Henkin, WA, *Bodywise – An Introduction to Hellerwork*. Wingbow Press, 1991

Hempfling, KF, *Dancing with Horses – Communication by Body Language*. JA Allen & Co Ltd, 2001

Hunt, VV, *Infinite Mind – Science of the Human Vibrations of Consciousness*. Malibu Publishing Company, 1996

Ingram, H & Winch, AJ, "Re-defining the Focus of Workplace Learning". *International Journal of Contemporary Hospitality Management*, Vol 14 No 7, 2002

Irwin, C, *Horses Don't Lie – What Horses Teach Us about our Natural Capacity for Awareness, Confidence, Courage and Trust*. Souvenir Press, 1998

Jaworski, J, *Synchronicity – The Inner Path of Leadership*. Berrett-Koehler, 1998

Jones, FP, *Body Awareness in Action – A Study of the Alexander Technique*. Schocken Books, 1979

Kets De Vries, M, *The Leadership Mystique – A User's Manual for the Human Enterprise*. Pearson Education Ltd, 2001

LeShan, L, *Cancer as a Turning Point – A Handbook for People with Cancer, Their Families and Health Professionals*. Penguin Books, 1989

McTaggart, L, *The Field – The Quest for the Secret Force of The Universe*. HarperCollins, 2001

Manz, CC & Sims, HP Jr, *The New Superleadership – Leading Others to Lead Themselves*. Berrett-Koehler, 2001

Markova, D, *I Will Not Die An Unlived Life – Reclaiming Purpose and Passion*. Red Wheel/Weiser, 2000

Mulligan, J & Griffin, C, *Empowerment Through Experiential Learning – Explorations of Good Practice*. Kogan Page Ltd, 1992

Oliveira, N, *Reflections on Equestrian Art* (translated by Phyllis Field). Hyperion Books, 1999

Olivier, R, *Inspirational Leadership: Henry V and the Muse of Fire – Timeless Insights From Shakespeare's Greatest Leader.* The Industrial Society (now Spiro Press), 2001

Oriah Mountain Dreamer, *The Invitation.* HarperSanFrancisco, 1999

Oshry, B, *Seeing Systems – Unlocking the Mysteries of Organizational Life.* Berrett-Koehler, 1996

Parelli, P, *Natural Horse-Man-Ship: The Six Keys to a Natural Horse-Human Relationship – Attitude, Knowledge, Tools, Techniques, Time, and Imagination.* Western Horsemanship Inc, 1993

Pert, CB, *Molecules of Emotion – The Science behind Mind-Body Medicine.* Touchstone, 1999

Petersen, VC, "Judging With our Guts – The Importance of an Ineffable Social Grammar". Working paper 99-12, Department of Organization and Management, The Aarhus School of Business, Denmark. 1999

Petersen, VC, "Making the Leap of Faith Part 2 – From Modern Management to Spirited, Value-based Leadership". CREDO/department of Organization and Management, The Aarhus School of Business, Denmark. Working Paper 2000 - 7. 2000

Rashid, M, *Horses Never Lie – The Heart of Passive Leadership.* Johnson Books, 2000

Reason, P & Rowan, J, *Human Inquiry – A Sourcebook of New Paradigm Research.* John Wiley & Sons, 1981

Rifat, T, *Remote Viewing – What It Is, Who Uses It and How To Do It.* Satin Publications Ltd, 2001

Rilke, RM, *Letters to a Young Poet* (translated by MD Herter Norton). WW Norton & Company, 1993

Roberts, M, *Horse Sense for People – The Man Who Listens to Horses Talks to People.* HarperCollins, 2001

Rogers, CR & Freiberg, HJ, *Freedom to Learn* (third edition). Prentice Hall, 1994

Rolf, IP, *Rolfing – Re-establishing the Natural Alignment and Structural Integration of the Human Body for Vitality and Well-being.* Healing Arts Press, 1989

Russell, EW, *Report on Radionics: Science of the Future – The Science which can Cure where Orthodox Medicine Fails*. The CW Daniel Company Ltd, 1994

Shaw, P, *Changing Conversations in Organizations – A Complexity Approach to Change*. Routledge, 2002

Smith, S, *Inner Leadership – Realize Your Self-leading Potential*. Nicholas Brealey Publishing Ltd, 2000

Stacey, RD, *Complex Responsive Processes in Organizations – Learning and Knowledge Creation*. Routledge, 2001

Stacey, RD, *Strategic Management and Organizational Dynamics –The Challenge of Complexity* (third edition). Prentice Hall, 2000

Thompson, JA & Bunderson, JS, "Work-NonWork Conflict and the Phenomenology of Time". *Work and Occupations*, Vol 28, Issue 1. 2001

Weil, S,"From the Other Side of Silence – New Possibilities for Dialogue in Academic Writing". *Changes, Special Issue: Tensions and Dynamics in Qualitative Research*, 14, 3 (223-231). 1996

Weil, S, "Social and Organizational Learning and Unlearning in a Different Key – An Introduction to the Principles of Critical Learning Theatre (CLT) and Dialectical Inquiry (DI)". *Systems for Sustainability: People, Organizations and Environments*. Stowell, F, Ison, R, Armsonet, R *et al.* New York, Plenum:373-381. 1996

Whyte, D, *Crossing the Unknown Sea – Work as a Pilgrimage of Identity*. Riverhead Books, 2001

Whyte, D, *The Heart Aroused – Poetry and the Preservation of the Soul at Work*. The Industrial Society (now Spiro Press), 1999

Permissions

Thanks to the following for their kind permission to quote from their publications:

Quotation from *Reflections on Equestrian Art* by Nuno Oliveira, copyright 1976, JA Allen, London, UK. Reprinted with permission of the publisher.

Quotation from *The Invitation* by Oriah Mountain Dreamer, copyright 1999, HarperCollins Publishers, London, UK. Reprinted with permission of the publisher.

Quotation from *Letters to a Young Poet* by Rainer Maria Rilke, translated by MD Herter Norton, copyright 1993, WW Norton & Company Ltd.

Quotation from *Crossing the Unknown Sea* by David Whyte, copyright © 2001 by David Whyte. Used by permission of Riverhead Books, an imprint of Penguin Group (USA) Inc.

Poem *I Will Not Die an Unlived Life* by Dawna Markova with permission of Conari Press, an imprint of Red Wheel/Weiser, Boston and York Beach ME. To order call: +44 1-800-423-7087.